W9-BFG-851

# Library Robotics

## THIS ITEM DOES NOT CHECK OUT

# Library Robotics

*Technology and English Language Arts Activities for Ages 8–24*

Sarah Kepple

LIBRARIES
UNLIMITED™
An Imprint of ABC-CLIO, LLC
Santa Barbara, California • Denver, Colorado

Copyright © 2015 by Sarah Kepple

**Library of Congress Cataloging-in-Publication Data**

Kepple, Sarah.
  Library robotics : technology and English language arts activities for ages 8–24 /
Sarah Kepple.
     pages cm
  Includes bibliographical references and index.
   ISBN 978-1-4408-3558-2 (paperback) — ISBN 978-1-4408-3559-9
(ebook)  1. Libraries—Activity programs.   2. Robotics—Study and teaching—
Activity programs.   3. Technological literacy—Study and teaching—Activity
programs.   4. Language arts.   5. Educational technology.   6. Young
adults' libraries—Activity programs.   7. Children's libraries—Activity
programs.   8. School libraries—Activity programs.   I. Title.
   Z716.33.K47 2015
   027.62'6—dc23        2015022334

ISBN: 978-1-4408-3558-2
EISBN: 978-1-4408-3559-9

19   18   17   16   15     1   2   3   4   5

This book is also available on the World Wide Web as an eBook.
Visit www.abc-clio.com for details.

Libraries Unlimited
An Imprint of ABC-CLIO, LLC

ABC-CLIO, LLC
130 Cremona Drive, P.O. Box 1911
Santa Barbara, California 93116-1911

This book is printed on acid-free paper ∞
Manufactured in the United States of America

AASL Standards for the 21st-Century Learner excerpted from *Standards for the 21st-Century Learner* by
the American Association of School Librarians, a division of the American Library Association, copyright ©
2007 American Library Association. Available for download at www.ala.org/assl/standards. Reprinted with
permission.

ISTE Standards for Students, Second Edition, © 2007, ISTE® (International Society for Technology in
Education), iste.org. All rights reserved. Reprinted with permission.

*For Mom and Dad, my first and greatest teachers*

# Contents

# Illustrations

## Figures

## Tables

# Preface

I was first introduced to the idea of educational robotics in 2008 when the central youth services department at Cuyahoga County Public Library booked a number of external presenters to align with that year's summer reading theme related to science, technology, engineering, and math. Stepping into the second day of a week-long day camp, I was amazed to see middle school students unabashedly geeking out and working in teams that cut across cliques and demographics to include diverse members. They were throwing around terms like *bushing*, *axle*, *beam*, *peg*, *gear*, and *sensor* with ease. They were writing and downloading programs to little robots that they'd made out of LEGO® bricks and adding custom components to move "moon rocks" or take a measurement on the Mars themed game board. I knew instinctively that THIS WAS IT. This was the solution for which I had been looking.

In the preceding years, working with youth in school and public libraries, I noticed how those who were often most at risk of not meeting their full potential would use the library as a third space, a hangout that was neither home nor exactly school. Through my work as a Treu-Mart Youth Development Fellow at Case Western Reserve University, I realized that what I wanted to do was foster resiliency, or the ability to bounce back from adversity. As a librarian, I couldn't control every factor in a young person's life. Bad things were going to happen to these students, but I could provide some support to help them become more resilient. I could provide each student with a supportive adult role model, an opportunity to use time constructively, outlets for creativity, enticing books to read for pleasure, and a community of encouraging peers.

At the same time, I was frustrated by the lack of real access to technology that many of these students faced. Few school systems then or now have the capacity for one-to-one computing, and these students suffered greatly from their only access often being a 30-minute session on a public workstation in the library. Students often needed help just to get to their favorite game websites. How was I ever going to help them get the technology skills that they would need to be self-supporting lifelong learners, let alone gainfully employed and involved members of a digital society?

Fast-forward back to my epiphany at robotics camp. I called the then manager of Youth Services, the inspirational Dr. Celia Huffman, and gushed about what I was witnessing. I asked if the library could get some robots, so that staff could continue this awesome learning. "Oh yes," she said, "We just received a grant." This was phenomenal news! I asked if I could be involved in the initiative. The response came quickly and would change the course of my career, "Absolutely! You're going to be in charge of it."

Since then, I have spent countless hours teaching robotics classes, sorting kits, leading staff development, and supporting colleagues and clients. At every professional conference at which I present, I am amazed at how instantly most attendees get it. As a library profession, we have embarked on an increasingly universal path toward active learning. In our spaces, we are making, exploring, researching, and publishing. At every venue, however, certain questions continually arise. Why robots? What does this have to do with books and reading? How am I supposed to do this and everything else? We bought robots, now what?

In this book, I attempt to answer some of these very valid questions. I am fortunate to have help in this regard from a number of professionals throughout the library and education community who have contributed their valuable perspectives. I have been inspired by their stories, as I hope you will be, and I am grateful to all who have helped forge this innovative path.

# Acknowledgments

This work has been greatly inspired by the incredible accomplishments of fellow professionals who have bravely blazed the robotics trail in libraries. Many thanks to the following innovators who shared their stories: Amy Georgopoulos, Beth Barrett, Bob Loftin, Christy Cochran, Kelly Czarnicki, Megan Alabaugh, Michael Cherry, Ryan Paulsen, Tara Radniecki, Tod Colegrove, PhD, and the awesome team of the Robot Test Kitchen: Heather Booth, Kim Calkins, Jacqueline Christen, Sharon Hrycewicz, and Michelle Kilty. Also, even though he's not a librarian, Tad Douce totally rocks too.

Gratitude is also due to LEGO® Education for their generous permission to use the screenshots that help illuminate possible solutions. Many thanks in particular to Stephan Turnipseed, Trisha McDonell, and Ivery Toussant, Jr., for their support.

This journey wouldn't have been possible without the five-star team at Cuyahoga County Public Library. Thank you in particular to Sari Feldman, Tracy Strobel, and Wendy Bartlett for your encouragement to write this book, to my friends and colleagues on the Robotix Team, to Julia Boxler and Dave Bullock for helping me storm the castle on more than one occasion, and to Celia Huffman, PhD, my incredible mentor and friend who started and supported me on this path.

Lastly, many thanks are due to all of my friends and family, who have put up with this and all of my other crazy ideas. I would especially like to thank the BDLs, the Club G crew and, most especially, Andrew Harant. You are all rock stars.

# Introduction

One of the most common misconceptions about leading robotics education in libraries is that the librarian must be an expert in all elements of the technology, but what surfaces repeatedly in conversations with colleagues who successfully lead robotics classes, camps, or clubs is a confidence not in their high-end computer programming or engineering knowledge, but in the certainty that their work is having a positive impact. They are experts in building relationships with customers and helping them find the information they need to do creative and innovative things. This is exactly the spirit with which to use this book. Set aside any concerns about using the technology and consider the possibilities to help grow literacies.

There are numerous existing resources available to help users learn any particular robotics technology or programming language, for those who are so inclined, so rather than overlapping and focusing too much on the technical nitty-gritty, this work focuses on the specific needs and educational goals of librarians. The intention is to help library professionals understand the benefits of using robotics in a library setting and start an initiative by using the sample budgets, logic models, and activity guides within. Use this work to learn how to build literacies with robotics, not to learn to code.

A few terms may need some clarification. Public librarians may be accustomed to using the word *program* to describe educational and entertainment events they host. That usage of the word is completely avoided throughout this work to avoid confusion with its meaning as it relates to robotics and computers, that of a sequence of coded instructions. It is also avoided because library *program* feels a bit passive for the very active learning intentionally happening in the classes and events described. Public librarians may not always consider themselves teachers, but in the examples provided within, they are certainly educators.

Of course the term *librarian* itself can be a bit controversial. This work welcomes all who work in a library who are willing to take up the causes of traditional and technology literacy to claim the term when it appears in the text. The terms *instructor*, *coach*, and *facilitator* are used interchangeably in the activity guides and may refer to the librarian or whoever is leading the event. Lastly, the word *student* is used to refer to anyone who is participating in the robotics learning, rather than only to youth. The hope is that we are all perpetually students.

Chapters 1 through 4 provide foundational background about why a library might want to use robotics, what types of robots are available, how other libraries are currently using robotics, and how to convince stakeholders and funders to buy in. Chapters 5 through 7 provide guides to present three different robotics events. When reviewing each guide, it may be useful to view the downloadable materials as they are mentioned. The links for all are in the Appendix.

# CHAPTER 1

# Why Robots?

In this chapter, we'll discuss what robots are and how using them as an education tool can increase multiple literacies.

## What Is a Robot?

Though generations of humans have pondered mechanical creatures, metal men, and automatons, the word *robot* first appeared less than a century ago in the 1920 hit play *Rossum's Universal Robots* by Czech playwright Karel Čapek (Markel, 2011). Since that time, popular culture has been fascinated with robots both benign and malicious. From the Jetsons's motherly maid Rosie, to human-hunting "squidies" in *The Matrix*, to the romantically inclined WALL-E, we just can't get enough.

Although most robots in literature and film are far more sentient and humanoid than the car-building and floor-sweeping robots of reality, they do share a few attributes. Surprisingly, there is no one official definition of what makes a robot a robot, but most tend to have the following in common:

## Brain

Thinking is what distinguishes a robot from a machine. A *machine* is a device that performs a task when given power. Robots also use power and mechanical parts to perform tasks, but unlike a machine, *robots* are programmable and autonomous or semi-autonomous. So, a basic toaster is a machine because its mechanical parts have been constructed to depress and heat the toast when turned on and stop when a timer triggers a release. Whereas, a Roomba® floor vacuum is considered a robot because it must take in information about the room and make decisions about which direction to go next. It is programmed with a logical test, and its thinking might go something like this, "Is there something in front of me? If so, back up and turn, if not, keep moving forward."

## Senses

Just as humans and animals use senses such as seeing, hearing, tasting, smelling, and touching to learn about and interact with the world, so robots need sensors to take in information. Robot sensors pick up physical stimuli such as light, heat, sound, pressure, or movement. A perennial favorite program of robotics students is reminiscent of the late 1980s phenomenon The Clapper®, a device that uses an electronic sound filter to "listen" for loud noises and responds by turning an electrical device on or off. In robotics class, we might attach a sound sensor to a robot and program it to start and stop moving when the decibel level of a noise registers above a certain threshold.

## Response

So, once our robot has used its sensors to take in data, and that data routes through the brain circuits, we expect something to happen. Whereas humans might have automatic responses to stimuli that are hard-wired into our brains, robots' responses must be programmed. Just as we might train a dog to sit every time it hears a command and sees a treat, we would program the robot to respond with a specific action to a certain set of stimuli. Just like the dog, the robot would not only need senses to be able to take in the stimuli and the brain to interpret the stimuli, it would also need the body parts to achieve the brain-triggered response. If a robot is programmed to insert bolts into a car frame every time one comes within a certain distance on the assembly line, it will likely need a rotating mechanical arm of some sort to achieve this response.

## What Do Robots Have to Do with Literacy?

Librarians who've experienced Brian Selznick's groundbreaking work *The Invention of Hugo Cabret* will doubtless remember the pure wonder and joy felt when the automaton produced a drawing seemingly from magic. Perhaps it is this magic, the group animation of individually inanimate parts, that captivates us about robots. No matter their age, those witnessing robots in action, or better yet programming them, invariably find themselves in a bit of awe. But, with everything else libraries must achieve today, with typically very limited funding, being cool may not be enough to warrant the investment required to create and sustain a successful robotics initiative. Robots can, however, be more than just another flashy gizmo or service and can instead be powerful tools to nurture literacy.

Ask any 10 educators to define literacy, and you'll get 10 different definitions. *Merriam Webster's Collegiate Dictionary* defines *literacy* as simply, "the quality or state of being literate." To be literate can mean to be "able to read and write," to be "versed in literature or creative writing," and/or to "have knowledge or competence."[1] In libraries, we regularly support literacy on all levels, from helping little ones build early literacy skills in storytime, to helping classrooms of children select reading material that both stretches and engages them, to teaching computer and database skills, to creating new media content. We wear many hats as we serve reading literacy, computer literacy, information literacy, new media literacy, and so many more. In this section, we'll take a preliminary look at how robotics can be used to support two particular types of literacy, English Language Arts Literacy and Technology Literacy.

# English Language Arts Literacy

English Language Arts Literacy might be considered *traditional literacy,* as it includes the types of skills that are typically the foci of school curricula such as reading, writing, and communicating. Often, traditional literacy has been primarily concerned with the technical ability to read and write, particularly as it relates to an individual's ability to participate in society and fully function in the workforce. Many advocate a more progressive definition, with librarians leading the charge. In fact, well before the emersion of the Common Core, the American Association of School Librarians (AASL) developed their Standards for the 21st Century Learner, which recognizes that for students to be fully literate, students must not only be technically able to read and write, but they must be inquisitive, read for pleasure, draw founded conclusions, and share knowledge effectively with others through various media.

Now, educators throughout the United States are shifting gears in line with the Common Core State Standards for English Language Arts (CCSS-ELA), which also promote a more holistic, inquiry-based learning methodology to produce students who not only can read and write, but also comprehend, interpret, and communicate. These standards emphasize text complexity, academic vocabulary, and content-rich nonfiction, and they encourage integrating literacy learning into other subject areas such as science, history, and technical subjects.

The CCSS-ELA employ *anchor standards* in Reading, Writing, Speaking and Listening, and Language. These four headings are composed of subgroupings of individual anchor standards, which are then further translated into grade-level appropriate standards. For the purposes of this overview, the subgroupings are summarized and addressed as succinctly as possible. Subsequent chapters will provide specific techniques and cite the standards for which activities were designed, but let's look a little at why and how robotics supports English Language Arts Literacy via these anchor standards.

## College and Career Readiness Anchor Standards for Reading

The anchor standards for reading fall under four main headings: *Key Ideas and Details, Craft and Structure, Integration of Knowledge and Ideas,* and *Range of Reading and Text Complexity*. An important concept of the Reading standards, and indeed the entire Common Core, is in the interrelated nature of learning. CCSS-ELA Anchor Standards for Reading include the following in a Note on Range and Content of Student Reading, "By reading texts in history/social studies, science, and other disciplines, students build a foundation of knowledge in these fields that will also give them the background to be better readers in all content areas" (2014). For example, discovering and applying practical physics and math concepts in robotics class might ground young readers as they embark on a complex and abstract journey through space and time with Meg, Calvin, and Charles Wallace in a *Wrinkle in Time*. Likewise, reading about how Ender thinks through his daily challenges at Battle School may inspire robotics students to approach problems differently and come up with unique solutions.

*Key Ideas and Details:* These standards are about identifying and citing important details and using them to make logical conclusions about the central concepts of a text and the root causes of events, development of ideas, and motivations of characters. Working with robotics requires focused attention to detail and interpretation of occurrences. Have a robot that's not doing what you think it should? Time to check through each element of the program for a detail that's off. Need some help developing a program? You'll need to be able to read through someone else's documentation, harness the key elements, build off of them, and analyze and explain your findings to your teammates.

*Craft and Structure:* In this grouping, the most obviously supported standard is about understanding word meanings from context. While there are certainly technical manuals that define most elements of robotics, most learning happens through tinkering and personal learning networks. Significant vocabulary growth happens rapidly as students learn by doing. Anxious to make their robots do something cool, they are motivated to seek out and retain the information needed in the moment, and accrue comprehension of terminology as they use it.

*Integration of Knowledge and Ideas:* These standards emphasize the role of reading as a lifelong learning and research tool and stress the need to be able to effectively interpret and analyze content in multiple formats on varied subjects. The further goal is for students to be able to assess how well a text's claims are supported with evidence and how it compares to other texts on the topic. This group of standards is essentially addressing research skills in the age of the Internet, when a sensory landslide of information makes careful discernment of credible and relevant sources vital. In addition to text in blogs and articles, that information now bombards students in the forms of videos, charts, graphs, icons, and GIFs, so not only must students be savvy at evaluating sources, but they must also develop visual decoding dexterity. As part of a participatory, connected learning environment, robotics students regularly pursue self-motivated, contextual research in order to solve problems, and they often go even further by contributing their own videos, blog posts, and forum submissions to the field. Because much of these data are quantitative, including numbers, settings, and code language, students are able to test sources and develop evaluative skills through trial and error.

*Range of Reading and Level of Text Complexity:* The emphasis on students tackling challenging texts, both fiction and nonfiction, permeates the Common Core. This imperative emphasizes stretching students not only to read at their highest technical level, but also to read broadly, from a diverse range of cultures and eras and in all subjects. It is common for robotics students to regularly and independently seek out complex informational texts about programming languages, coding techniques, engineering strategies, and more, but this research can extend well beyond direct instructional and informational materials into literary nonfiction that provide broader background. In fact, the robotics competition juggernaut FIRST (For Inspiration and Recognition of Science and Technology) includes a research project so that FIRST® Lego® League teams can investigate and problem-solve real-world scenarios. To gather context for a challenge based on solving problems caused by natural disasters, students might read background articles on geology and oceanology, historical journal entries about floods in the area, and scientific reports about the impact of global warming. Whether for a competition or class, the opportunity to use robotics to engage students with high-level reading is vast.

# College and Career Readiness Anchor Standards for Writing

The anchor standards for writing are divided into four main categories: *Text Types and Purposes, Production and Distribution of Writing, Research to Build and Present Knowledge,* and *Range of Writing*.

*Text Types and Purposes:* These standards center around effectively using appropriate techniques to write persuasive, informative, and narrative texts. This includes well-reasoned and evidence-based arguments, organization and clear expression of information, and creating logical and well-developed plot sequencing. The Common Core emphasizes argumentative writing, not from a desire to produce students who can win any argument, but to push students to root their opinions and interpretations in fact, an important tendency for those both inside and outside academia to develop. Teams of robotics students research and experiment to solve problems, but part of collaboration is being able to articulate and support envisioned strategies to the rest of group. By maintaining discussion boards and contributing to forums, robotics students can practice and develop evidence-based writing. By creating blogs about the team's progress, setbacks, and experiences, students develop event sequences and build narrative skills.

*Production and Distribution of Writing:* These standards focus on the planning and editing process, designing works to suit a particular intention and audience, and, notably, connecting with others by publishing and discussing works via technology. As mentioned in the previous standards, deep robotics learning invariably encourages, even requires, participation in an online, global community. Though much of this engagement is informal, there is an opportunity to harness students' enthusiasm for robotics and direct it into using writing process fundamentals such as planning, revising, and editing to create fully composed articles whether for the local newspaper, a guest blog, website, or trade magazine.

*Research to Build and Present Knowledge:* Of particular interest to librarians, these standards speak to Information Literacy skills such as forming good research questions, locating and assessing sources, and using gathered information to support writing and personal understanding of the subject researched. Even if robotics students aren't participating in a competition that requires a background research project or marketing and business research, developing research skills is fundamental to connected and participatory robotics learning.

*Range of Writing:* This heading has only one standard, "Write routinely over extended time frames (time for research, reflection, and revision) and shorter time frames (a single sitting or a day or two) for a range of tasks, purposes, and audiences." This standard aligns with robotics learning, though it does require some diligence from the educator, since, at its heart, this standard is about habitual, regular writing, which according to research such as the 2010 Graham and Hebert report *Writing to Read: Evidence for How Writing Can Improve Reading* supports improved reading. Conveniently, the practice of writing often aligns with the best practice in computer programming of documenting sections of code for later referral, explanation to colleagues, or reminders of the rationale behind them.

# English Language Arts Standards for Speaking and Listening

The CCSS-ELA Anchor Standards for Speaking and Listening include *Comprehension and Collaboration* and *Presentation of Knowledge and Ideas* as well as the following Note on Range and Content of Student Speaking and Listening:

> New technologies have broadened and expanded the role that speaking and listening play in acquiring and sharing knowledge and have tightened their link to other forms of communication. Digital texts confront students with the potential for continually updated content and dynamically changing combinations of words, graphics, images, hyperlinks, and embedded video and audio.

The wide availability of video communication tools such as Skype, Google Hangouts, and YouTube has been one of the greatest disruptive forces to how we learn and think about learning. Educators looking to harness this power are experimenting with *Flipped Learning*, assigning students the homework of watching video-recorded lessons that they can pause, rewind, repeat at their own pace, and then using classroom time for projects, collaboration, coaching, and interactivity. Public and school librarians are exploring *Connected Learning* which, among other things, democratizes education, bringing peers and experts into dialogue and collaboration, often through online media.

With new opportunities come new challenges, however, and the CCSS-ELA Anchor Standards for Speaking and Listening take into account that graduating students will need skills to present TED talks, connect and collaborate with colleagues in different time zones and from different cultures, and cipher out facts from an avalanche of media and messaging. As we'll see, robotics provides a perfect opportunity to practice and develop these types of skills amid a diverse, international, and online community.

*Comprehension and Collaboration:* Communicating and working well with others, one of the main foci of progressive education theories such as 21st Century Skills and Connected Learning, also finds a home in the Common Core. The Comprehension and Collaboration standards for Speaking and Listening recognize that students will be entering a global workforce and must be able to understand and grow from a diverse range of ideas, across multiple media formats, while effectively expressing themselves and assessing the point of view and validity of other speakers' arguments. By now, it's probably clear from the previous anchor standards just how central collaboration is to the team learning and group dynamics of robotics. Team members must articulate their own ideas and build off the ideas of others, find a balance between skepticism and encouragement, and create and evaluate code, drawings, written plans, and data. There are few learning opportunities that could surpass robotics for supporting comprehension and collaboration.

*Presentation of Knowledge and Ideas:* These standards focus on planning and articulating rationally constructed presentations, effectually using supportive multimedia, and tailoring the message to the setting and audience. Robotics provides numerous opportunities to develop and practice presentation skills. Competitive teams may create pitches for potential sponsors, class groups might present findings from background research, and clubs could create and share instructional videos for fellow enthusiasts. Even in a stand-alone class in a public library, students can create mini presentations to show what they've learned to family and friends after the program.

# English Language Arts Standards for Language

The first two categories of CCSS-ELA Anchor Standards for Language, *Conventions of Standard English* and *Knowledge of Language*, are probably supported in a less direct fashion by robotics than the other standards, unless, of course, the robotics leader makes a concerted effort to focus on conventions and effective language usage. However, these skills are intertwined with those of reading, writing, speaking, and listening.

*Conventions of Standard English:* These standards emphasize competent usage of standard English grammar in writing and speaking. It's unlikely that a robotics class or public library club would devote significant time to *direct* instruction on this topic; however, one of the unique emphases of the Common Core is the interconnectedness of learning and providing rigorous support. To put it simply, when writing for robotics class students should employ the same attention to grammar, syntax, and spelling as they would if writing for English class. As we've seen in the reading, writing, and speaking standards above, with robotics there are plenty of opportunities to get students communicating about a subject they love.

*Knowledge of Language:* This standard emphasizes rich use of language, interpretation of nuances, and full comprehension when reading or listening. This is a complex standard, and the topics emphasized in each grade vary widely, including everything from word choice to precise and concise writing to style manuals. With such a wide range of skills to consider, it is certain that, with the breadth and depth of communication options in robotics learning, students will have the opportunity to further develop their knowledge of language.

*Vocabulary Acquisition and Use:* These standards focus on gleaning the full meaning(s) and nuances of words and phrases from context and reference materials and demonstrating self-driven acquisition of vocabulary in all subject areas and personal interests. One of the more impressive powers of robotics learning is building vocabulary from context. Within the first few hours of robotics classes, students begin correctly using terms like "bushing," "axle," and "calibration," and much of this is from independent investigation and contextual understanding. Whether students eventually work professionally in STEAM fields or not, this vocabulary expansion and tendency to independently improve their own lexicons can help them achieve on ACTs, fearlessly face academia and the work force, and better understand the world around them.

# *Technology Literacy*

Unlike Math and English Language Arts, there are currently no Common Core State Standards for technology itself, though the Common Core encourages integrated technology learning. Some of the agencies that have been most influential regarding concepts of Technology Literacy include the International Society of Technology in Education (ISTE), the International Technology and Engineering Education Association (ITEEA), the AASL, and the Partnership for 21st Century Skills (P21). All these organizations have produced standards that support technology literacy. Though they scale from very specific industrial technique to broader cognitive skills, all share common themes around the participatory and investigative process of building and growing technology literacy.

Two of the standard sets that may be most familiar to educators in the technology, library, and literacy fields are the ISTE Standards, previously titled the National Educational Technology Standards (NETS), and the AASL Standards for the 21st Century Learner. Both resources were published in 2007; however, they are broad enough in regard to mechanical skills and specific enough about cerebral growth to retain their vibrancy today. Following in the footsteps of Margaret Mead's great adage that "Children must be taught how to think, not what to think," these standards aim to help students become critical thinkers and problem solvers who are intellectually curious and able to enthusiastically adapt and embrace new technologies as they emerge. As with the English Language Arts standards, subsequent chapters and activity plans will reference specific technology standards as they apply, but let's look at how robotics supports the broad context of Technology Literacy. For efficiency in this overview, the AASL and ISTE standards, found in their entirety on their respective websites, have been grouped together and summarized into five main areas of consensus or complimentary approaches.

## Creativity and Curiosity

*ISTE: 1. Creativity and Innovation: Students demonstrate creative thinking, construct knowledge, and develop innovative products and processes using technology*[2]
*AASL: 4. Pursue Personal and Aesthetic Growth*[3]

It is, perhaps, no surprise that the very first ISTE standard is *Creativity and Innovation*. After all, the point of learning any foundational skills, whether they be coding basics, math operations, English grammar, or elements of the periodic table, is not really to regurgitate them on a test, but to use them as building blocks for creating new content and discoveries. In no discipline is this more true than in technology, a field in which innovations over the last 10 years alone have dramatically changed our culture. Futurist Ray Kurzweil argues in his 2001 essay on the Law of Accelerating Returns that if we continue at our current rate of technical progress, "We won't experience 100 years of progress in the 21st century—it will be more like 20,000 years of progress." The stunning advances we've experienced in biomedical fields, nanotechnology, and more are a direct result of the intellectual curiosity and creativity of researchers, inventors, designers, and educators.

In its similar standard, *Pursue Personal and Aesthetic Growth*, AASL encourages students to take in everything: read books, watch videos, listen to the world, and connect ideas. Seek out information, organize what you've learned, and share it through all manner of creative ways. Never before in human history have so many people had access to so much information. Access alone, however, isn't enough. Students must demonstrate insatiable curiosity. AASL describes an indicator of ideal student disposition as exploring beyond school requirements. This sentiment is further echoed in the work of the Connected Learning environments of the MacArthur Foundation's YOUMedia spaces, which advocate the power of interest driven learning, particularly as it intersects with academic content and is supported by inspiring peers and the openly networked tools of the digital age.

Real-life, touchable, interactive robots invariably capture the interest of any and all who encounter them, in part because the human eye is attracted to motion, but as Howard and Holcomb discovered in their 2010 research, the human eye is particularly drawn to unexpected changes in motion. This makes sense as our fight or flight primordial instincts wouldn't know if a being changing direction suddenly was coming to attack us or bring us food, but either situation was worth our attention. Robots are one of the few nonliving things with the potential to engage us in this way. Perhaps this is why a robotics demonstration never fails to capture the absolute attention of every student present. Once students find their interest naturally piqued by witnessing a robot in motion, the next question is invariably, "can I try?"

After naturally triggering curiosity, robots provide unlimited opportunities for creativity as students find original ways to solve complex problems through programming and design. For instance, when students working with LEGO® MINDSTORMS® are challenged with moving a ball from one location to another, each is likely to create a slightly to wildly different solution. One team might build an attachment that rolls the ball beside the robot as it moves, another might build an arm that hits the ball like a golf club, and still another might create a scoop that picks the ball up and carries it. Even if two teams apply the same strategy, their designs might be completely unique. With robotics challenges, there is no one "right" answer, so the space for creative innovation is infinite.

# Communication and Collaboration

*ISTE: 2. Communication and Collaboration*
*AASL: 3. Share Knowledge and participate ethically and productively as members of our democratic society.*

As we discovered in the English Language Arts Literacy section, robotics provides numerous opportunities for building communication and collaboration skills. Due to the cost of robots, few libraries or schools could provide a 1:1 robot to student ratio, and most would avoid doing so. Students who work together to design, build, and program a robot must be able to clearly articulate their own ideas, but they are also highly motivated to listen to the ideas of others as the group brain is typically able to solve the challenge better and faster than any one individual. It is also common in a robotics class for students to peer coach each other and share ideas. When a student or team discovers something new, other teams invariably ask "How did you do that?!," and the proud young engineers are delighted to show all. Even in competitions such as FIRST, it is common to see teams showing good sportsmanship by lending each other tools, time outs, parts, and person power.

Even the rare and lucky student who has his own robotics kit at home is likely to participate in a vibrant online community. AASL's standard *Share Knowledge and Participate Ethically and Productively as Members of Our Democratic Society* encourages students to participate in personal learning networks beyond academic settings and to "create products that apply to authentic, real-world contexts." Though some robotics projects may have more practical applications than others, students who create instructional videos, blogs, and online instructions not only increase their own understanding of the components of the project by explaining it to others, but they also build communication capital. The skills necessary to explain complex building or programming methods in an accessible manner, and to participate in democratic online environments such as forums, resound with future employers in a global economy. ISTE recognizes this as well, for one of their *Communication and Collaboration* standards is "Develop cultural understanding and global awareness by engaging with learners of other cultures." The universality of elements found in robotics, including math and coding, provides an opportunity for not only multicultural communication, but multilingual as well.

## Critical Thinking and Problem Solving

*AASL: 1. Inquire, think critically and gain knowledge*[4]
*ISTE: 4. Critical Thinking, problem solving and decision-making*[5]
*ISTE: 6. Technology Operations and concepts*[6]

It may strike some as odd that both ISTE and AASL avoid endorsement of specific technologies, computer skills, or coding languages, but considering the exponential pace of advancement, creating such explicit guidelines would render them obsolete before they could even be completed. Not only is technology developing too rapidly to be quantified, cataloged, and standardized, but the future of work also remains a hazy mystery. To paraphrase Sir Ken Robinson in his now famous 2006 TED Talk: Children born today will be retiring in 2065, and no one has a clue what their future will hold, but we're meant to be preparing them for it. We are no longer the industrialized nation the traditional education system was designed to support, a system that expected and hired individuals to fill certain predetermined rolls. Now, the world of work is changing so rapidly that future-minded educators are focusing as much on the how as the what. The 2010 National Education Technology Plan asserts that, "Whether the domain is English language arts, mathematics, sciences, social studies, history, art or music, 21st Century competencies and such expertise as Critical thinking, Complex problem solving, Collaboration, and multimedia Communication should be woven in all content areas." Regardless of the work our youth will grow up to do, the global, interconnected world will demand these "4 C's" as much if not more than the "3 R's." By helping students develop critical thinking and problem solving skills, we are preparing them to encounter any new technology with impunity and empowering them to be their own educators.

Students working with robotics become steadily immersed in a culture of people who view obstacles with the joy of an athlete facing a worthy opponent. In fact, both VEX and FIRST robotics competitions use the word *game* to describe the set of trials and the parameters which they'll face. Librarians who've explored badging may already be familiar with the concept of *gamification*, a term referring to the utilization of game elements to increase engagement. Although the elements of competition, prizes, and levels might be used, the spark to transform something difficult to something fun might be as simple as semantics. Consider how differently one might view a *riddle* versus a *word problem*.

Robotics provides many opportunities to create game-like environments that motivate students to build problem solving and critical thinking skills as they gain knowledge about technology. As noted in the CCSS Reading standard group for Key Ideas and Details, students evaluate what is needed, plot a course, and diagnose errors. When challenged to make the robot climb a structure as quickly as possible, students might begin by thinking up critical questions. How much weight does the structure hold? Will our proposed building solution weigh less than that? If not, how can we adjust it without losing functionality? Because each team's robot may be slightly to very unique, each team must find unique solutions to problems. Is the robot drifting to the left when it moves across the floor? You'll need to check whether it's due to something in the program code or the robot design, or both, and problem-solve how to fix it.

All of this rich critical thinking and problem solving happens concurrently with technological skill building. Students quickly and consistently must "troubleshoot systems and applications," one of the ISTE standards for Technology Operations and Concepts. If one of a robot's programs stops working after updating the operating system, a team must troubleshoot whether the issue lies in the OS, the program, or both. Often troubleshooting requires researching multiple components of the technology (utilizing the CCSS-ELA standards discussed above) and building greater understanding of how each one functions. Of course, over time, students learning one programming language, robotics product, or technique will gain enough competence to easily "Transfer current knowledge to learning of new technologies," yet another component of ISTE's Technology Operations and Concepts standards.

## Information Literacy

*ISTE: 3. Research and information fluency[7]*
*AASL: 2. Draw conclusions, apply knowledge to new situations, and create new knowledge[8]*

In synergy with the Integration of Knowledge and Ideas CCSS Reading Standard, the AASL and ISTE information literacy standards emphasize the ability to locate, organize, analyze, evaluate, and use information, and, though they say it in slightly different language, both encourage this to happen in an inquiry-based process. As robotics students problem-solve challenges, they constantly create lines of inquiry, which they are highly motivated to investigate. This creates the perfect, energetic environment for librarians to guide students as they build information literacy. When Library Media Specialist Ryan Paulsen's FIRST Robotics Competition team was featured in *School Library Journal* in April, 2014, he perfectly reflected how librarians can mentor information literacy skills and intellectual curiosity through inquiry-based learning. "Even though I didn't have the technical skills, the fact that as a librarian, research is second nature to me, I would never get overwhelmed by the idea of learning or finding the information about how to do something." This is precisely the entrepreneurial spirit and can-do attitude that will help students be successful in and beyond school, and why AASL, ISTE, and the CCSS all emphasize these skills, which robotics learning can help grow.

## Digital Citizenship

*ISTE: 5. Digital citizenship[9]*
*AASL: 3. Share knowledge and participate ethically and productively as members of our democratic society[10]*

Like the CCSS-ELA Anchor Standards, the ISTE and AASL standards recognize the need for students to be able to fully engage with a diverse digital world. This includes ethical issues such as avoiding plagiarism, understanding digital content licensing, and respecting intellectual freedom, as well as communication and collaboration behaviors such as seeking out and respecting diverse viewpoints and participating in personal learning networks and community discussions. As we saw throughout the CCSS-ELA Anchor Standards, robotics students have ample opportunities to engage with online learning communities and to "create products that apply to authentic, real-world contexts" (AASL 3.3.4). While many robotics challenges might be based on realistic scenarios, even using online venues to guide others through how to code something uniquely goofy offers students a glimpse at the modern lives of engineers, educators, and tech support personnel. Robotics students "Exhibit leadership for digital citizenship" (ISTE Digital Citizenship D) when they create and maintain websites for their FIRST teams, post how-to videos, redirect inappropriate behavior, or provide supporting documentation on discussion boards. Robotics learning provides librarians a rich playing field to help students become responsible and productive digital citizens.

# CHAPTER 2

# How Robots?

Now that we've established why robots have a place in the library, let's take a look at who's using them and how.

## Who Can Lead Robotics Learning?

Public, school, and academic libraries around the country are transitioning from book palaces to community learning centers that support creation and collaboration. Robotics fits right in with this technologically supported culture of making and doing, and there are numerous members of the library community who bring expertise. Whether knowledgeable in research, organization, design or, yes, computer programming, each person has a role to play.

## *Librarians*

The heart of any library, the frontline librarians and assistants bring a plethora of applicable traits, including research skills, technology expertise, and valuable community connections.

## Librarians as Information Literacy Educators

Regarding research skills, Murchison Middle School Library and Information Specialist Christy Cochran jokingly tells her students, "Just assume I know everything because I can find out how to get the information."[1] Though she laughs at the hyperbole, the importance of empowering students to research thoughtfully and document thoroughly may not be overstated. As examined in the first chapter, the CCSS-ELA, AASL, and ISTE standards all heavily emphasize the need for students to find, analyze, evaluate, use, and share information. All of the panel members who created these various standards had good reason to emphasize information literacy skills. In the digital age, success in work and personal endeavors relies less on memorization of facts and more on the ability to find and utilize ever-evolving information.

Cochran first became involved with the school's robotics program when she realized that the competitions required students to research topics relevant to the competition theme and present their findings. Cochran advises other librarians, "Don't wait to be invited!" Though the robotics coach may have initially been a little surprised when she volunteered to help the team improve their research strategies and presentations, he was receptive, and the team benefited tremendously. Not only did the students significantly strengthen their information literacy through the experience, but when they told the judges about their library learning, they also received major kudos and bonus points.

Like many librarians, New Rochelle High School Library Media Specialist Ryan Paulsen uses his passion and aptitude for research to master new technologies. Reflecting on his first hectic year as head coach of the New Rochelle Huguebots he observed, "As a librarian, I have such a command over the information gathering process that I could give myself a couple of seconds to find the information I needed."[2] Paulsen relied on that awareness as he dove head first into starting up a brand new FIRST Robotics Competition team. With only six weeks to pull together a team and build a functioning robot, Paulsen rapidly put students to work researching all elements of the competition, from marketing and strategic planning to detailed technical investigations and coding languages. Paulsen sees robotics as a perfect representation of the cross-curricular work of librarians, and he regularly partners with teachers who specialize in a variety of subject areas. Not surprisingly, teachers often seek him out as a technology coach, a role that many librarians have readily embraced. School and public librarians now regularly educate those they serve and create communities of learning around new technologies.

## Librarians as Technology Literacy Educators

Beth Barrett, Director of Library and Museum Services in Louisville, Colorado, views technology education as central to the library's mission. "It's become increasingly clear that there are all types of literacies. Traditionally, we think of reading, but STEM literacy is equally important." [3] She believes that integrating hands-on robotics and coding into the library's offerings is critical because, "Studies have found that experimental learning is how all of us, kids and adults, learn best, and sometimes that type of learning takes place outside of the classrooms. Public libraries are a perfect place for this to happen."

Dr. Tod Colegrove, Head of DeLaMare Science and Engineering Library at the University of Nevada, Reno, might argue that rich, experimental learning happens *best* in the library.[4] Since 2010, Colegrove and his staff have transformed their space by moving archived materials into storage and coating the walls with whiteboard paint to create 40–50 collaboration spaces, all of which are now in near constant use. His colleague, Engineering Librarian Tara Radniecki, explains that they've worked hard, not only to find out about students' interests, but also to express their own "geeky-ness." She says, "We're more than happy to have robots in the library . . . which happens more often than you might think."[5] One of the reasons it happens is because DeLaMare circulates robot kits and "micro-programmables" including MaKey MaKeys, Raspberry Pi, Arduino SparkFun Inventor Kits, Little Bits, and Pinocchio wireless microcontrollers. The library also provides software support, not only loading their computers with tools such as LEGO® MINDSTORMS®, Visual Studio, Visual C, and Photoshop, but also subscribing to Lynda.com a premium website home to thousands of video tutorials to support making.

Colegrove says that by the library staff "waving their geek-flag high" they've attracted not only students from the traditional STEM fields but also those from art and business majors. Now he sees a "rich froth of incredible minds bouncing off each other," including the minds of the library staff who support the constant inquiry-based learning. Colegrove says that the number of traditional reference questions has increased exponentially now that students see the librarians as part of a vibrant community of technology explorers.

Evansville Vanderburgh Public Library (EVPL) Teen and Youth Services Librarian Michael Cherry shares this vision of the library as a technology-learning center. He is interested in teaching robotics and digital media because, "We're in a culture that [is] consuming technology so readily, [but] we could be doing creative things with it and educating with it."[6] In fact, he says, one of EVPL's goals is to move beyond providing access and support of new technologies and to offer technology classes and learning opportunities in a way that's community focused. He notes that robotics has been a great unifier in this way because of the vast amount of industry in Evansville and throughout Indiana, the state with the highest share of manufacturing employment per capita, according to a 2014 report from the Bureau of Labor Statistics. Using his skills as an information professional, Cherry researches and shares industry examples to help students frame their robotics learning in real-world contexts. He reflects that using robotics with the students has made him more aware of the local industry and career opportunities. He predicts that due to the way things are changing, advanced technology skills are going to be important in every field, from design to medical, and he projects that with all that they're learning, "These robotics projects may end up landing a student a job someday."

## Community Volunteers and Partners

This type of drive and power to connect with the local community runs deep among librarians. Teen Services Librarian Kelly Czarnecki agrees that one way in which librarians are particularly suited to support robotics education is by using their community knowledge and connections. She explains that even though librarians may not always be the primary experts, "we have the community connections to know who is."[7] Cochran concurs. As a school librarian, she interacts with everyone on campus, from teachers, to students, to parents and support staff. Reflecting on how she is able to harness these relationships to create a connected learning environment for students, she says, "Working with me is like working with the community."[8] In the next section, we'll look at how libraries are recruiting community members to lead robotics learning.

### Robotics Teams as Partners

Designed as a collaborative, shared space of the Charlotte Mecklenberg Library and Children's Theatre of Charlotte, ImaginOn is built on a foundation of community partnership. This spirit continues in the robotics learning opportunities that Czarnecki enjoys with local organizations. In the summer of 2014, tinkerers and experts from Hackerspace Charlotte helped launch and run a Google Makercamp at ImaginOn, and some of their members have been regular contributors to ImaginOn's biweekly Robotics Club, which is predominately led by members of the YETI FIRST Robotics team.

Existing robotics teams are prime community resources because their members typically possess rampant enthusiasm and diverse technological skills. Additionally, robotics competitions such as FIRST and VEX® provide incentives to encourage teams to perform educational outreach. Robotics teams can lead interactive projects or bring the robots, which they've worked so hard to build, and provide demonstrations for the communities that support them. Other student organizations may also be good resources. Members of Theta Tau, a coed professional engineering fraternity, worked with Colegrove and Radniecki and the DeLaMare Science and Engineering Library to host International Arduino Day. The library provided the space and organization for the campus-wide event while the student fraternity members provided the expertise and person-power.

According to Barrett, the Louisville Public Library has hosted local teams for exhibitions, but they have also engaged adults in the community as Junior FIRST LEGO® League (JrFLL) mentors.[9] Former teachers and engineers have contributed their time and talents, and even the local fire department got in on the action, helping the students research the JrFLL theme about natural disasters and emergency preparedness. In addition to individuals, the Louisville Public Library's long-standing partnership with the Space Science Institute's National Center for Interactive Learning has led to several exhibit installations, including a Discover Tech exhibit that left behind several Snap Circuits kits. These kits now circulate to help library customers learn about basic circuitry.

## Partners from Academia

Community partners may also provide professional development for librarians or other future robotics instructors. The University of Texas at Austin's Design, Technology, and Engineering for All Children (DTEACh) website explains that the program and Professional Development Institute "features integration of engineering design challenges into other disciplines . . . from literature to science and mathematics to art. DTEACh provides K-12 teachers with engineering design pedagogy and design-based, project-based, hands-on activities for teaching applied mathematics and science" (University of Texas at Austin, 2011). As an educator who sees firsthand how project-based learning can give students the opportunity to build collaboration and problem solving skills, Cochran highly valued her experiences in the DTEACh program, and she says that it also helped her build a comfort level with the LEGO® MINDSTORMS® kits and programming environment.

A little further north in the state, the Plano Public Library (PPL) partnered with the Science and Engineering Education Center (SEEC) at the University of Texas at Dallas to launch their robotics program. According to Municipal Reference Librarian Bob Loftin, at the request of PPL Director Cathy Ziegler, the SEEC created and trained staff on the eight-week Rockin' Robotics curriculum. The SEEC even lent PPL the LEGO® MINDSTORMS® robotics kits and laptops.[10] After a year of library staff leading Rockin' Robotics throughout the system, Ziegler applied for and received a grant to purchase the library's own robot sets and laptops. Loftin and colleagues from each of the five branches formed a committee and generated new ideas, and now branches are experimenting with a wide variety of models.

EVPL also benefitted from academic sponsorship. According to Cherry, in January of 2012 Ivy Tech Community College (ITCC) received funding from Alcoa, Inc. to launch a robotics outreach program. Community organizations were invited to apply, and accepted groups, including EVPL, each received a VEX® kit and 15 hours of advisor training in exchange for agreeing to sponsor a team for three years for the Novice competition. Cherry says that the initial training was invaluable as was the greater robotics community and network of support that ITCC created.[11]

Of course, some of the best human resources in the community may already be in the library or on the campus according to Colegrove and Radniecki. Since transforming the DeLaMare Science and Engineering Library into an active experimental space, Colegrove says that it is common to see faculty stopping in to interact with groups of students. The students themselves also serve as resources. Reflecting on the anxiety that sometimes surrounds new technology, Radniecki observes, "Librarians get scared of not knowing everything, but I give [students] power and respect by saying, 'That's awesome! Can you teach me?' "[12] Colegrove and Radniecki also regularly employ the time-tested librarian art of referral by keeping abreast of happenings on campus and in the community and connecting students to mentors who can help them take their personal and collegiate interests to the next level.

## Community Educators

Though libraries may be one of the best places for students to learn outside of the traditional classroom, they are not the only place. Science centers, government agencies such as NASA, museums, and corporate outreach departments all may be resources for libraries to investigate when looking for external presenters. Additionally, libraries may be able to contract with agencies offering robotics education as a service. This can be a good way to maintain finite costs and allocate resources while the library runs robotics classes on a trial basis.

Cuyahoga County Public Library began what would become, quite possibly, the largest librarian-led robotics model in the country by bringing in a local technology education company to lead classes throughout the system. Librarians at each of the 27 branches were then able to gain some experience and personal interest. Data about the overwhelming community response supported requests for grant funding to grow the library's capacity for robotics education.

# How Can Library Robotics Work?

Each librarian interviewed for this book offers a model that functions uniquely in some way. From drop-in events to day camps to competitive teams, the ways in which libraries are using robotics are as varied as the libraries themselves. In this section, however, we'll explore some of the most universally shared approaches.

## Stand-Alone Classes and Events

A common model for public libraries, stand-alone classes offer the most scheduling flexibility and are relatively inexpensive. Libraries concerned about offering access to the greatest number of students may offer multiple date options of a stand-alone class and only prepare once. Stand-alone classes are also used to spark interest in robotics at special events and during outreach.

Every library has a slightly different approach. When students from the neighboring middle school were considering putting together a robotics team, Rocky River Public Library Teen Librarian Megan Alabaugh led an introductory session to introduce them to programming. She also offers periodic exploratory sessions in which teens play with building and programming robots using guides in the LEGO® MINDSTORMS® kits and tutorials in the software.[13] Plano Public Library also offers these types of freestyle sessions for teens as well as Family Robotics, which invites parents and children to play and learn together with LEGO® WeDo® kits. Loftin also leads Bob's Robot Apocalypse, in which students navigate robots through a wrecked city.

Cuyahoga County Public Library (CCPL) offers stand-alone classes throughout the school year. These mini sessions use selected challenges from their week-long summer camps, but the two-hour classes fit into busy after-school and weekend schedules. Staff members who have just recently begun learning to lead robotics are encouraged to cut their teeth on these abbreviated programs. Each rookie librarian is paired with an experienced mentor. The partners work together during a hands-on staff development session, then the mentor leads a class for students with the rookie's assistance. Each new staff member, therefore, receives the opportunity to student teach before leading her first class, during which the mentor serves as the rookie's assistant. This system helps nurture skill and assuages anxiety among new robotics instructors.

Stand-alone programs may also be used as an outreach tool. Michael Cherry gets extra mileage from the VEX® Swept Away set, which EVPL received through grant funds, by taking it to area schools for robotics demonstrations.[14] Schools that may not have the funds to purchase expensive, innovative technology welcome the opportunity for the library to provide access to their students, and the library appreciates the chance to introduce students to the world of learning available to them at the public library.

As mentioned in the previous section, public libraries might also *receive* outreach from local robotics teams. By inviting robotics teams in to lead exhibition programs, public libraries can offer their communities exposure to the world of robotics while also celebrating the achievements of local students. These relatively simple, one-time interactions can lead to broader partnerships. In 2012, ImaginOn partnered with the YETI Robotics Team, a FIRST robotics competition team made up of teens from the surrounding community, to host a Kick Off celebration for the FIRST LEGO® League program. Approximately 75 attendees attended volunteer-led workshops and presentations, including a sneak peek at that year's challenge field and access to topical experts. This event sparked a connection that would lead to the reoccurring Robotics Club discussed later in this chapter.

# Camps

Many public libraries have begun offering day camps, particularly during the summer, to keep students productively engaged during out-of-school time and to ward off summer slide—the loss of knowledge and skills that happens when students' brains are left idling for three months. The New York State Library and California Library Association websites provide annotated bibliographies of some of the best and most recent entries in a vast body of research to support the assertion that reading and participating in educational events at the library reduces or eliminates summer slide.

CCPL's robotics camps provide just this type of engagement. Students work in pairs to build and program LEGO® MINDSTORMS® robots that tackle challenges faced by characters in popular books. For instance, in a camp based on Jeff Kinney's first *Diary of a Wimpy Kid* book, students read about "the cheese touch" and then must program their robots to navigate around a piece of cheese placed in the center of an activity board. The camps are typically held for a maximum of 12 students and run two hours a day for four days. At the end of the week, students demonstrate their challenge solutions to an audience of family and friends and earn points for each challenge completed based on difficulty. Camps are designed for varying age-level groupings based on the selected book title and may include youth from 7 to 18 years of age.

EVPL camps differ somewhat, though the class size is kept similarly small, with a registration limit of 12–15 students. Coming to the library two hours a day, once a week for four weeks, students must use their time wisely to figure out how to complete a challenge at a mini competition at the end of the four weeks. The beginner camps use LEGO® MINDSTORMS® kits as students are typically comfortable building with LEGO® bricks and can therefore concentrate on learning how to program. Advanced camps use VEX® kits which require greater building skill and are navigated by remote control rather than autonomous programming.

ImaginOn's 2014 Google™ Maker Camp offered students aged 13–18 a chance to play with robotics components such as circuits, power sources, and programming. Over the course of six weeks, students could dabble with MaKey MaKey™ invention kits, Arduino™ Uno circuit boards, copper tape, coin cell batteries, LEDs, and more with the help of members of Hackerspace Charlotte. With no registration and a casual drop-in atmosphere, each student could customize his or her own experience, learning from the adult mentors, the provided *Make:* magazines or Google+ videos.

# Competitions and Clubs

For some, the term *competition* may be as synonymous with robotics as it is intimidating. As evidenced by the previous sections, however, forming a competitive team is only one way to approach robotics learning. Though some librarians directly coach competitive teams, others serve as research mentors or provide opportunities for outreach. Other libraries replicate the atmosphere of geeked-out fellowship that competitive teams provide by offering ongoing or reoccurring clubs.

## Jr. First LEGO® League

Librarians looking for a gradual start into the world of competitions might consider the Jr. First LEGO® League (Jr.FLL), says Beth Barrett.[15] In 2013, the Space Science Institute's National Center for Interactive

Learning notified the Louisville Public Library's Director about the opportunity to pilot a Jr.FLL program in an effort to see how the program could work in public libraries. Barrett says that often leagues are formed in schools with students who already know each other, but bringing the program into the public library opened up participation to the larger community and provided a chance for students to connect with others who shared their interests.

Barrett says that in their first year the library organized five teams of students aged six to nine. Each team had access to a LEGO® kit. Teams, coached by community volunteers, met for two to three hours a day, once a week at the library for six weeks. After researching the 2013 topic of natural disasters, students created models and posters to show a solution to how a community might recover. Unlike the other FIRST programs, the Jr.FLL does not require programmable robotics components; however, each team's model must include at least one motorized part. The simple machine in each model might include ramps, pulleys, axles, wheels, gears, and other such elements. At the conclusion of the six weeks, the library held an exhibition at which students presented their projects to a panel of local judges and community. Reflecting on the experience, Barrett glows, "That was a great day!" The library filled with people who were excited to see what the students had done. With the overwhelming community response, and the enthusiastic support of the children's librarians, Barrett looks forward to continuing Jr.FLL in years to come.

## FIRST Robotics Competition

On the opposite end from Jr.FLL on the FIRST program spectrum is the FIRST Robotics Competition (FRC) for high school students. Each year FIRST reveals a new FRC field design and challenge and then FRC teams have six weeks to build a robot from scratch to compete on a life-sized field. During this six-week build period New Rochelle High School Library Media Specialist and FRC Huguebots Team Advisor Ryan Paulsen[16] says that his team meets daily after school in the library.

At the competitions, matches take place between alliances, each composed of three robots, each robot representing one team. The teams of each alliance work together to score the most points, although Paulsen asserts that, "Once you really know what's going on, the competition aspect isn't really important." He says that participating in the event is "transformative and so addicting," adding, "It's the most fun sporting event you'll ever go to!" Like all FIRST programs, students participating in FRC are held to a high standard of *gracious professionalism®*, a term coined by Dr. Woodie Flowers, *FIRST* National Advisor, and Pappalardo

Professor Emeritus of Mechanical Engineering, Massachusetts Institute of Technology. Students demonstrate gracious professionalism by treating others with respect and courtesy even in the midst of fierce competition. Paulsen says that the most prestigious award to win by far is the Chairman's Award, which holds up a team that best exemplifies the values and goals of FIRST such as mentorship and helping others.[17]

In the Teen Loft of Charlotte Mecklenburg Public Library's ImaginOn, the YETI FRC Team demonstrates this spirit on a bi-weekly basis during the team's off-season. Visiting students have the opportunity to join the team in exploration of robotics components using items like MaKey MaKey kits and paper circuits to learn about programming and circuitry. The team may also bring a puzzle for students to solve that involves using the library's LEGO® MINDSTORMS® robots. According to the YETI Robotics website, the team is composed of high school–age public, private, and homeschool students from throughout the area and is dedicated to promoting robotics learning through outreach, as Kelly Czarnecki learned during their successful partnership on the FIRST LEGO® League (FLL) Kick Off event. This partnership gives the team the opportunity to develop new skills, maintain knowledge, and build camaraderie, and it brings high-level peer-to-peer learning into the library.

## Library Robotics Clubs

In addition to providing support to their peers, students may also provide guidance to professional staff. The tween and teen members of CCPL's Robotix Advisory Team test draft challenges for upcoming camps, offer feedback and suggestions, and recommend classes on topics of interest to their peers. The young advisors are invited to join the team based on their demonstrated programming or building skill and their observed ability to communicate and collaborate well with others in a previous camp or class. Made up of students from throughout the county, the team typically meets quarterly at a central location, with additional meetings to prepare for summer camps. The Information and Technology Literacy Specialist, who oversees CCPL's Robotix Blox initiative, organizes and hosts the meetings that provide her invaluable insight.

Several CCPL branches also run local clubs, which vary in structure, but are typically geared toward youth aged seven through ten. At the monthly sessions, library staff lead the students through lessons using the LEGO® WeDo® robotics kits and Extension Activities. A few of the branches also run LEGO® MINDSTORMS® based robotics clubs for older students. These are typically quarterly and may use challenges from the camps as launching points to inspire students to explore and create their own models. In the summer of 2014, BonesBOT, one of the camps offered system-wide and based on the book *The 39 Clues: Maze of Bones*, was designed by teens in the Southeast Branch's robotics club.

# VEX® Robotics Competitions and FIRST LEGO® League

Of course, libraries are not necessarily required to choose between clubs and competition teams. Since 2012, EVPL has fielded a VEX® robotics team as part of the Ivy Tech Community College's local Novice competition. Each year ITCC designs a new game and then sends teams the objective(s), rules, and pictures of the playing field. For instance, in the 2012 Slippery Slope game, contestants had to climb a ramp while directing 16 golf balls into various locations. In the 2014 Marco Polo game, the driver of the robot was hidden behind a curtain and was guided by another member of the team. Cherry says that the structure provides a great deal of creative freedom with each team taking a different approach and designing a unique robot.[18] Teams present their robots to the judges, describing the process of how the members designed, built, and modified their projects. Inspired by their setting and the resources they had explored with Cherry, the EVPL team presented their robot by creating an original graphic novel, much to the delight of the judges.

Cherry says that after receiving the initial VEX® kit through the ITCC program and seeing the fantastic learning happening and overwhelming public response, the EVPL decided to expand beyond the competition team to offer seasonal clubs. A new club begins each quarter, and registered students in grades 6 through 12 participate for two hours a day, one day a week for six weeks. Like the competitive team model, the club activities are cumulative. Students are divided into teams that work on a culminating project, and they are afforded the opportunity to explore beyond the competition by researching relevant topics and real-life robots as well as playing with other types of robots and challenges. In a future club, Cherry plans to use LEGO® MINDSTORMS® robots and the LEGO® Education Green City challenge kit which invites students to investigate clean energy solutions and build models using wind and solar energy.

Murchison Middle School also offers a combination of clubs and teams, although as the Library and Information Specialist, Christy Cochran has primarily been involved as the team's research coach. Initially, Cochran worked with the members of the FLL team. As in the junior version, FLL teams are given an annual topic. In addition to building and programming a LEGO® MINDSTORMS® robot that will complete challenges based on the topic during the game portion of a competition, the students, in grades 4 through 8, must research the subject and present a project. According to the FIRST LEGO® League's participation rules, the project must "identify a problem, develop an innovative solution," and the team must share their solution with others (FLL, 2014). To complete the project, students must research not only the topic, but also the preexisting solutions to the problem, as well as organizations, companies, or groups who may wish to hear about their solution. Additionally, they may be researching ways to share their solution such as how to build a website, create a blog, publish a letter to the editor, or write a newspaper article.

After helping the school's FLL team achieve their research and presentation goals, Cochran was an obvious resource for the VEX® robotics team when they started up the following semester. The Robotics Education and Competition (REC) Foundation presents the annual VEX® Robotics Competition (VRC), which is open to middle school, high school and postsecondary students. There are several different ways to participate in VRC. One member from each team may compete in the Robot Skills Challenge, in which the driver plays alone against the clock. The Programming Skills Challenge is played with an autonomous robot using sensors, and there are several other Online Challenges involving Computer-Aided Design (CAD), animation, essays, and more. The main event, however, is The Game in which standard matches consist of two alliances, each composed of two teams, playing against each other. In addition to competing in the game and other challenges, teams who wish to be considered for the Design Award or the most prestigious Excellence Award at the VEX® World Championship must submit an Engineering Notebook.

According to the REC Foundation, engineering notebooks "provide teams with a document of their design decisions." (RECF, 2014) In their review, judges are particularly interested in content relating to "project, budget, resource and time management." Cochran reflects that while, as a librarian, she has a great deal of technical skill, her most valuable contribution to the team has been to push students to take a broader view. With the notebook, she encourages students to explain their reasoning, show the research and work that has led the team to a decision, and consider the audience for whom they are writing. Cochran says that she has had a tremendous opportunity to help build students' ELA literacies through both the FLL Project and VRC Engineering Notebook elements. She further emphasizes that the project-based nature of robotics learning is the perfect environment for students to develop research, communication, collaboration, and problem solving skills that will benefit them across all subject areas.

# National Robotics Challenge

Another competition that libraries may wish to consider is National Robotics Challenge (NRC). According to NRC Director of Events and Tri-Rivers Educational Computer Association Director of Innovation and Development, Tad Douce, the Society of Manufacturing Engineers originated the event in 1984 to create a talent pipeline.[19] That concept continues in NRC with competitions for students as young as third grade all the way through college. There are a variety of events each requiring various levels of skill and time commitment, but Douce thinks what really recommends NRC to libraries is the minimal cost involved and the openness of the platform. With no specific kit to buy, participants can be as innovative as possible, as cheaply as possible.

# Further Considerations

Whether through stand-alone classes, camps and series, or competition teams and clubs, libraries can use robotics to connect with their communities and build literacies. Factors determining which solution is the right fit might include staffing time and initiative, community specifics, and the physical space available.

# *Staffing*

The amount of staff time required for robotics offerings varies greatly, from a few hours of organization and marketing to host a robotics team demonstration to several weeks of preparation and presenting for librarian-led camps and clubs. Those librarians interviewed who are involved with competitions emphasized the need to allocate a lot of time and manage it well. In his first year as head coach of the New Rochelle Huguebots, Ryan Paulsen had to hit the ground running, trying to help students in daily meetings while simultaneously educating himself on all the intricacies of building, programming, and FRC. Now in the second year, Paulsen still meets with some members of the Huguebots team daily during the six-week build season, but only with those members who are contributing to the specific task at hand. Out of season, the team meetings drop from daily to biweekly and from 3 hours to 50 minutes.[20] This particularly high level of time commitment may be particular to teams who are building robots from scratch and competing in advanced level competitions; however, from her experience with FLL and VRC, Christy Cochran also advises fellow librarians to make sure that they are properly prepared to dedicate themselves to a significant time commitment. She is quick to point out, though, that once an organized program has been established, "it kind of runs itself."[21]

That's not to say that robotics learning doesn't require a librarian with drive. All of the librarians interviewed were successful in their work at least in part due to their tenacity and willingness to learn. Administrators looking to launch robotics on any scale within their libraries should look for a library staff member with initiative to head the efforts and support that person on his or her quest.

Cuyahoga County Public Library's robotics program grew to its current scale due in large part to the dedication of the central Youth Services Manager to advancing STEAM and 21st Century Learning opportunities in libraries. Through her leadership, external presenters were booked to lead demonstrations and summer programs. Through this initial exposure, a staff member was identified who possessed the interest and dedication to create what would become the Robotix Blox model. This Specialist worked with an initial action group of eight Children's and Teen Librarians who were also tapped for their enthusiasm, to create a stand-alone, staff-led model. After testing and tweaking this class, the action group identified eight new librarians to join the effort. This "each one, teach one" approach has continued under the Specialist's guidance so that over 60 youth librarians have now been touched and can lead robotics programming in their respective branches. To be successful, this approach needed buy-in and support from all involved including administrators, branch managers, the Specialist, and youth librarians.

Loftin acknowledges staff buy-in as crucial to the success of a robotics initiative. He encourages libraries that are starting out to involve staff members who are eager, regardless of job title. As Municipal Reference Librarian, he wouldn't typically be involved in offering classes in the branches, but his director recognized his interest in the topic and technological aptitude. Likewise, Loftin recognizes the strengths his colleagues bring. "I'm continually blown away by just how masterful our youth services staff are. One of the greatest skills they bring is their ability to connect with a room full of kids."[22] Regardless whether the skills they contribute are digital or interpersonal, staff members who are enthusiastic will make the enterprise a success.

Libraries that need to develop excitement might be best served by starting small with an externally presented event or a simple, stand-alone class. Similarly, school libraries with one, already stretched librarian or small libraries with limited staff might consider a creative scheduling approach like Haslet Public Library in Texas. After the library received ALA's Loleta D. Fyan Grant, Youth Services Librarian Amy Georgopoulos was faced with the challenge of creating a successful robotics initiative within the very limited staffing hours available. Although Georgopoulos says that she would prefer to run camps four days in a row, she needs to balance the camp with the other staffing needs of the library, so the camp runs on the day of the week with more staff for four consecutive weeks.[23]

## Community

Georgopoulos also advises fellow libraries to consider their specific communities before selecting an approach to robotics. At the time that the grant was written, Georgopoulos says that the library was aware that the local high school was involved in competitions, but they did not realize the extent to which elementary and middle school students were gaining exposure in the school's Techno camps. Once Georgopoulos learned about the camps, however, she seized upon the opportunity. While volunteering for the camps, she grew her own knowledge and developed a better understanding of how the library's offerings might complement those of the school system. The library's camps focus more on teamwork and critical thinking rather than on the technical skill and competition.

Local need also drives EVPL's Michael Cherry. He encourages librarians who are considering starting a robotics initiative to identify a community driven focus around which to center the students' learning.[24] While in Evansville, that focus may likely be around some of the resident manufacturing industry and their use and development of robotics, other communities might develop robotics series that help students who are struggling with math or reading skills. Libraries with large new adult populations in their cities but not their libraries might develop robotics clubs as a way to connect with the 18–24-year-old crowd. In communities that are already rich with robotics offerings, the library might be a central meeting place, host of a regional tournament, or a research partner to area teams.

## Location, Location, Location

Though the physical space required depends more on the type of robots selected than it does on the type of educational model, the availability of a physical space may be an important consideration. A stand-alone class or limited series may be easier to arrange for libraries short on meeting space than an ongoing club, though librarians willing to think outside the meeting room box may find creative solutions. Once Paulsen understood the size of the robot that his team would be building, he realized that there were few options in his overpopulated school. There was, however, one space over which he had complete scheduling control: the school library, so the area became a true makerspace, with students building, programming, and testing the robot right on the public floor.

Another point to consider when selecting a model is whether students will need to travel to another location to participate in any events. It is typically relatively practical for school librarians, acting under the jurisdiction of the school to arrange transportation of students to competitions and events off campus. Public libraries, however, differ dramatically in their policies on the issue. It may be feasible for public librarians to meet students at a location even if they cannot transport them there, but each library should seek legal council on the issue.

The obvious consideration that many readers may be questioning is cost. Though some might find it surprising, the librarians interviewed expressed very few concerns about funding, regardless of the scale of their operations. In the next chapter we'll explore why that might be, and how libraries might select robotics materials and find the money to pay for them.

# CHAPTER 3

# Which Robots? Selecting and Paying for Equipment

The two most common questions asked by librarians who are considering entering the world of robotics education are, "How much?" and "Which robots should I get?" The two questions rely on each other for answers and are influenced by a myriad of other factors such as educational goals, age, or developmental level of the students, space availability, and funding solutions. In this chapter, we'll explore some of the options and how they align with these considerations.

## Robots for Sale

In the early days, educators interested in introducing students to robotics had few options other than building their own from scratch. The costs involved and the expertise required typically prohibited all but the most well-funded, highly skilled experts from doing so. Now, with the abundance of cheap and powerful electronic components available, and the national emphasis on STEAM learning, numerous vendors are supplying the market with robotics products that are accessible to the average user.

It was, in large part, a desire to help librarians sort through these ever-expanding options that inspired a five-member team to create the Robot Test Kitchen website as their iLEAD project. The group of youth-focused librarians wanted to create a resource for librarians who were interested in expanding their libraries' STEAM learning options through robotics. Says Heather Booth, Teen Services Librarian at Thomas Ward Memorial Library, "We wanted to be very authentic in our reviews—the kind of stuff that we would want to know before purchasing [a product]."[1] The team members ordered a variety of robot products, tested them in the library with their students, and then wrote honestly and frankly about their experiences. Reviews include practical details such as target age level, battery life, the type of setting for which the robot is best suited, durability, and cost. Though the project timeline has now concluded, the team plans to continue their work, and the Robot Test Kitchen website continues to serve as a great resource for librarians to explore resources and connect with others who share their interests.

Like the initial project of the Robot Test Kitchen, this book is designed primarily for those who are new to robotics or who are exploring robotics as one of many library responsibilities, so the items featured in this chapter are either prebuilt, "program and play" robots or robots that may be built from a kit with minimal tools. With so many options entering the market daily, the task of creating and maintaining a comprehensive guide to every available robot falls outside the scope of this work. Though there are many other effective options, the robots listed in this chapter have been selected for their viability in library settings, and their capacity to help students build multiple literacies. The robots are divided into three categories: Entry-Level, Novice, and Intermediate. Though some robots may lend themselves better to certain age users, the categories speak more to the skill required by the user and facilitator. It is not, however, necessary to begin at the Entry-Level. All of these products may certainly be entry points and self-taught through enough perseverance and research.

## Entry-Level Robots

Many adults watching toddlers manipulating tablets or teens texting at lightning speed assume that these behaviors demonstrate an inherent ability with technology that skipped their own generation. In *The Salmon of Doubt*, iconic author Douglas Adams addresses this sentiment: "I've come up with a set of rules that describe our reactions to technologies: 1. Anything that is in the world when you're born is normal and ordinary and is just a natural part of the way the world works. 2. Anything that's invented between when you're fifteen and thirty-five is new and exciting and revolutionary and you can probably get a career in it. 3. Anything invented after you're thirty-five is against the natural order of things."[2]

To succeed with the following entry-level robots, adults (even those over 35) might consider emulating the littlest learners. Touch, observe, learn, and repeat. Says Downer's Grove Public Library Children's Reference and Technology Coordinator Sharon Hrycewicz, "It's okay to fail forward. To make a mistake, but keep going."[3] After daring to dive in and try out robotics as part of her work with the Robot Test Kitchen, Hrycewicz says she's learned to, "step back, let [the students] take control. Before, I felt that if I didn't know how to do this, they would look at me like a failure, but I believed in the process. I found that it was okay. I've bought in." She advises other librarians to take a step back and "know that it's okay. If it doesn't work, that's okay, that's how kids are learning." The entry-level robots in this section are designed for just this type of self-driven, exploratory learning that allows for librarians and students to dive in and start playing.

## Bee-Bot™

Designed for the littlest learners, the Terrapin Bee-Bot, not surprisingly, looks like a bumblebee. The Bee-Bot technically does not sense anything, and would, therefore, fall short of the typical definition of a robot. However, the large scale, friendly design makes it accessible to the littlest learners, and the ability to program simple sequences makes it a valuable tool for early literacy skill building.

*How It Works:* There are four directional keys on the hard plastic shell of the Bee-Bot: forward, back, right, and left. Students may use these directional keys as well as the pause key to enter a sequence and then push the go button to activate. An additional button clears the previous program and prepares the Bee-Bot to receive a new sequence. The Bee-Bot blinks and flashes after each step, so users can follow along with the sequence.

*Age-Levels:* The design of this product obviously targets students in early childhood, and children as young as three are likely to be successful.

*Costs:* Purchased from the manufacturer's website, the Bee-Bot retails for approximately $90. There are optional additional accessories such as mats and lesson plans.

*Usage:* This is a great tool for those working with early readers. Librarians can buy or create a paper alphabet board and challenge the students to move to the letters of their names. Students could also "draw" letters or shapes using the Bee-Bot, or older students might program the Bee-Bot to follow the sequence of a story. There are also numerous opportunities to build math literacies; for instance, using a grid matt or taped outline, students can play with basic graphing.

With such young students, the hands-on aspect becomes even more critical, so ideally, there should be a one-to-one ratio of robots to students. The setting could vary from an extension activity during or after storytime, to a station during a family event, to an on the floor or bookable toy. Even if only one Bee-Bot were available, a librarian could lead students through creating a sequence as a group using their words or printed action cards.

## Cubelets

According to manufacturer Modular Robotics, "Cubelets are magnetic robot blocks that snap together to make an endless variety of robot toys." The appeal is almost as much about what is absent as it is about what is present, as no external programming or wiring is required.

*How It Works:* Each block is preprogrammed with certain capabilities. The user arranges the blocks in different configurations to simultaneously build and program a robot. Following the three main components that make a robot a robot, there are three main categories of blocks: Sensor Blocks, Action Blocks, and Think/Utility Blocks. The Cubelets Six Kit comes with two of each type of block as well as a Brick Adapter which allows users to connect Cubelets with LEGO® bricks or other similar construction sets.

*Age-Levels:* Modular Robotics recommends Cubelets for ages four and up. The building block design certainly makes these accessible to little learners, but with 16 additional blocks, the Brick Adapter and additional accessories, there are numerous possibilities for older students as well. For instance: a teen or adult could build a car out of LEGO® bricks, connect the build to the Cubelet blocks with the Brick Adapter, and use the Bluetooth Block to remotely control the mobile machine via her tablet.

*Costs:* The Cubelets Six Kit markets for around $150. The Cubelets Twenty Kit is approximately $500, and the Educator Pack of 49 Cubelets is about $1,100. Cubelet blocks may also be purchased individually, and they are typically about $25 each, although some specialty blocks such as the Bluetooth Block may be substantially more. Only advanced users who wish to write original code using the Bluetooth Block will also need to provide a computer.

*Usage:* Cubelets are perfectly designed for individual, explorative play. In the library setting, this might work best as a station within a larger program, such as a family STEAM or robotics day, or as a kit available for in branch or home use. Keep in mind that every Cubelet robot requires at least one battery block, one action block, and one sensor block. A Six Kit probably best serves one person or a pair working as a team, whereas the Educator Pack includes 5 batteries, and enough blocks for 5 individual robots, or 10 students working in pairs.

The initial investment might be offset by the durability and universal appeal of the blocks. The Cubelets might be used as a station in a stay and play storytime in the morning, be available for in-library check out to teens hanging out after school, and then be a tool in an adult coding club at night. A school librarian rotating through a district could use the Cubelets with her kindergarten classes up through her high school classes. Jacquie Christen, Grade School Program Coordinator at Glenside Public Library, says that Cubelets work well in a lot of her programs in which tweens must also supervise younger siblings.[4] Though students may take their learning farther when encouraged by library staff, basic use of the Cubelets requires minimal guidance or expertise.

# Novice-Level Robots

It becomes increasingly difficult to categorize robots that are beyond the entry-level category because so many of them have low floors but very high ceilings in terms of capabilities. It may be relatively easy for a new user to achieve the basic functionalities of the robot; however, the product may be customized or elevated based on the exploration of the user or the way in which the facilitator employs it.

## LEGO® WeDo®

Few toys inspire as much trust and enthusiasm among students, parents, and educators as LEGO® products. The LEGO® WeDo® solution capitalizes on this by introducing students to robotics concepts such as engineering, design, and programming through the familiar tools of LEGO® bricks, and a simple, drag and drop visual programming software.

*How It Works:* Guides in the software and accompanying booklets help students build simple models out of the LEGO® WeDo® construction set. The accompanying teacher guide provides coached activities to explore simple and motorized machine concepts and vocabulary. The software also provides programming guides to helps students bring their models to life. For instance, students are able to build an alligator model that uses a sensor and motor to open and close its mouth when food nears. The models are connected to the computer, and manipulated via the drag and drop software, rather than downloaded to a separate "brain."

*Age-Levels:* LEGO® Education recommends LEGO® WeDo® for students in second through fifth grade.

*Costs:* A single LEGO® Education WeDo® Construction Set is around $130. A single software license and teacher's guide set is $90, or a site license, which typically covers installation on all of the purchasing institution's computers, is about $300. LEGO® Education offers a variety of packages that each include a number of construction sets and a software site license. The overall cost per student decreases based on the number of sets purchased. There are additional Extension Activity Packs available that focus on Science, Engineering, Math, Technology, Language and Literacy, and 21st Century Skills. Though materials may be ordered from the LEGO® Education website, interested libraries may receive special incentives and individualized support from a regional sales representative.

Ideally, each LEGO® WeDo® construction set should be paired with access to the software on a computer. Any additional computers purchased to support LEGO® WeDo® classes will need to be considered into the overall cost. The software is available for Windows or Apple Macintosh.

*Usage:* LEGO® WeDo® is designed for a participatory classroom, in which students work in pairs or small teams and are coached by an adult facilitator. The instructional videos embedded in the software provide a great deal of support, including both technical instructions for replicating the example program solution and challenges for students to customize and create their own solutions. With these tools, interested students might be able to experience some building and programming success without much guidance, such as in an open station; however, students are more likely to make broader STEAM, 21st Century, and literacy connections when gently coached by an adult.

Cuyahoga County Public Library uses LEGO® WeDo® robots in stand-alone classes, camps, and clubs. In all three models, students work in pairs and are guided by a library staff member. The Plano Public Library System (PPLS) offers a unique class in which families work together as teams under the guidance of a library staff member. Perhaps it's the familiarity of LEGO® bricks, or the simple usability of the software, but PPLS Municipal Reference Librarian Bob Loftin notes that some staff find the LEGO® WeDo® products more accessible than other products.[5] In her review for Robot Test Kitchen, Sharon Hrycewicz points out that students typically bring experience and skill with brick building, so the facilitator may concentrate more on understanding and explaining sensors and simple machine components.[6]

As Hrycewicz also points out, because the system is built on the LEGO® platform, the sky is the limit in terms of building and creativity. The pieces in the construction sets include the gears, axles, sensors, and motors necessary to build the models in the instruction guides, but libraries may use other LEGO® sets to expand options and give students additional challenges. For instance, students might be challenged to build a castle out of the library's regular bricks and then add a drawbridge, using the LEGO® WeDo® motor and sensors, that opens when a person on shore waves. Not only can the LEGO® WeDo® sets often provide this type of motorized function for the Junior First LEGO® League program, but they could also partner with LEGO® StoryStarter or regular building sets to help students create and tell stories using simple and motorized machines.

Librarians entering robotics education as a way to help introduce young children to programming, but without much experience themselves may find LEGO® WeDo® to be a good fit. The visual programming environment provides user-friendly instructions and a vast online LEGO® community provides a network of support.

# Sphero

Sphero looks a bit like a white bocce ball, although it can be programmed to glow other colors. It can be controlled remotely via a smartphone or tablet, used as a game controller, or programmed to function autonomously. According to the Sphero website, it is highly durable, both pet proof and waterproof.

*How It Works:* Sphero connects to mobile devices via a built in Bluetooth connection and a number of apps available via the Apple App Store, Google Play, and Windows Store. Says Heather Booth, "something I love about [Sphero] is that it works on so many levels. You can use it like a game controller. It has the augmented reality feature, which is fun, and then there's an app called Draw and Drive—which is really, I think, the best illustration of what computer programming is for young kids."[7] With the Draw and Drive app, users can draw a picture or path, using various colors and then press play to see Sphero drive what they drew. Booth appreciates how well this works at a basic, introductory level and that users can take it further, creating macros with more specific instructions and digging into autonomous programming.

*Age-Levels:* The multifunctional nature of Sphero makes it appealing to a variety of age groups from early elementary school through teens to new-adults and seniors.

*Costs:* The Sphero 2.0 lists at about $100. Worth considering is the roughly $20 Sphero Chariot accessory. It works a bit like a traditional chariot with the Sphero serving as the horse. The Chariot includes a built in slot for a mobile device to record the Sphero's movements and has nubs perfect for attaching LEGO® bricks. Though less applicable in the library setting, the Nubby covers, available in a variety of colors for about $15, help the Sphero go all terrain.

Of course, another associated cost with Sphero is the necessary compatible device. The Sphero website lists devices that have been confirmed to work with the interface. These range in price from a $180 Kindle Fire HDX through a plethora of Windows and iOS devices up to a $500+ iPad. If the library already owns devices, this may not be an issue, but keep in mind that each Sphero will need a device for them all to be used simultaneously. Note that not all apps are available on all platforms.

*Usage:* One of the tremendous benefits of Sphero is its versatility. Kim Calkins, Middle School Services Librarian at Elmhurst Public Library, brings Sphero out to the reference desk. She says a few minutes of driving it around the youth area creates a Pied Piper effect that's, "like shooting fish in a barrel."[8] Students gather around, take turns, and engage with her in an easy manner. This can be a great resource for youth librarians looking to connect with children, tweens, and teens in a nonthreatening manner.

Even though it is typically one student controlling the Sphero ball through one device, there are many ways to engage multiple students simultaneously. Jacquie Christen notes that one solution is to have students create obstacle courses for each other. Although there are a variety of predesigned Sphero games, such as a tag game, in which one student chases the others with the ball, Heather Booth has had students create their own games such as one student drawing with the Sphero, while the others guess the drawing.

Because of Sphero's low entry point, Christen points out that it's a great tool for empowering the community. Librarians can roll it out and let users create. Users may also choose to take their learning farther by exploring programming apps such as MacroLab, a basic visual environment, and orbBasic, a richer text-based environment. Librarians looking to offer traditional classes may wish to explore the Schools Parents Robots Kids (SPRK) lessons plans available from the Sphero website.

Because Sphero can be used as a remotely operated vehicle (ROV) or as an autonomous robot, it may also be an option for competitions, such as National Robotics Challenge, that place minimal restrictions on the types of products used.

# Intermediate-Level Robots

The robot products in this section may present a steeper learning curve for some, but they offer the opportunity to build custom and highly capable robots within a reasonable cost and learning curve.

## LEGO® MINDSTORMS®

Built out of a partnership between the LEGO Group and Massachusetts Institute of Technology, the original RCX "intelligent brick" was launched in 1998, according to the company website. Though some educators still use these yellow classics, most have transitioned to either the NXT, released in 2006, or the third and most recent version, the EV3, which was released in 2013.

*How It Works:* The three main components of LEGO® MINDSTORMS® Education are the programmable brick, the software, and the structural components including LEGO® bricks, sensors, and motors. Note that the Education EV3 Core Set, available online and through LEGO® Education sales representatives, contains slightly different components and uses a different software version than the EV3 Home Edition, which is sold in retail stores. The same type of programmable brick is used in both versions and will work interchangeably with parts and software from both. The following commentary refers exclusively to the education version.

The EV3 programmable brick, which serves as the robot's brain, includes a display, buttons to navigate and program via the interface, input ports, output ports, mini USB port, SD Card Port, USB Host port, and speaker. Unlike previous iterations, the EV3 Education kit also includes a rechargeable battery for the brick, though users may also choose to use AA batteries.

To create the body of the robot, users may follow building guides or design their own models using the Technic building bricks, motors, sensors, and cables included in the kit. Users may expand their builds with an expansion set, which is sold separately, or with their own bricks.

To activate the robot, many users program the brick either through the on-brick programming application, or by connecting the brick via USB or Bluetooth to a computer and downloading programs built in the standard EV3 Education software. The EV3 Education software is based on National Instruments' LabVIEW™, a graphical programming environment used by scientists, engineers, and industries that require a control system. LEGO® Education President Emeritus and Executive

Director of Strategic Partnerships Stephan Turnipseed points to the use of this industry standard, domain-level software as one of the many benefits of LEGO® MINDSTORMS® products. He offers the example of a researcher needing to keep lab tanks filled with a certain level of fluid.[9] Normally, it might take 10 pages of written code to turn a pump on, fill up a tank, determine how much fluid is in the tank, and keep it at a certain level. Using the LabVIEW™ software, he can create the program in four or five graphic blocks. This allows the researcher to remain focused on his own domain, or expertise, rather than becoming burdened with complicated programming. Likewise, librarians using LabVIEW™ may remained focused on their own domains of traditional and technological literacy and use the software as a tool to introduce students to robotics and the logic required for programming without having to become experts in coding.

That is not to say, however, that the software is overly limiting. On the contrary, Tad Douce shares the story of a former student who was selected for a prestigious college program involving diesel-electric trains because of his experience using LabVIEW™ on the LEGO® robotics team. Now the student is an engineer in the field. The usability of the software and the creative freedom of building with LEGO® bricks offers students an entryway to more complex programming if they are so inclined. LEGO® MINDSTORMS® intelligent bricks may also be programmed with RobotC, a gateway to coding with C, and many enthusiasts experiment with full-fledged, text-based languages.

*Age-Levels:* LEGO® Education recommends LEGO® MINDSTORMS® EV3 for those aged 10 and up. Given the popularity of LEGO® with adults as well as youth, and the near limitless extent to which the brick may be programmed and used, the "up" in this case truly refers to teens, new-adults, adults, and seniors.

*Costs:* A single EV3 Core Set with Charger lists at about $340. A single copy of the EV3 Software is about $100, and a site license is about $400. Like the LEGO® WeDo® kits, the exact price per student cost decreases with larger bundles. For instance, the 2014 LEGO® Education catalog advertises a package of four core sets and a site license for a little over $1,700.

It is possible to program these robots solely on the EV3 Brick itself; however, to take full advantage of the product's programming capabilities, libraries may wish to provide computers. The EV3 Education Software works on most recent Mac and Windows operating systems.

Those interested in creating metal robots may also wish to budget for Tetrix Building System materials, which are used in FIRST Tech

Challenge and other competitions. A TETRIX Education Base Set is approximately $600.

*Usage:* Because generations of learners find LEGO® products familiar and enticing, library users may welcome the ability to check out kits for independent, home exploration. An important point to consider, however, is the value of the kits and the management of a number of small pieces.

Many potential users will need additional support, and the potential for in-library learning abounds. As discussed in the previous chapter, libraries throughout the nation use LEGO® MINDSTORMS® in stand-alone, series, camp, and club models. Classes may vary from basic, introductory sessions that introduce users to building and programming using the standard software and guides to competition style games to advanced coding clubs. Facilitators new to LEGO® MINDSTORMS® may wish to attend one of the typically inexpensive workshops provided by LEGO® Education and organized by regional sales representatives, though the tutorials available in the Robot Educator portion of the software may be sufficient for some. Additionally, a vast online network of educators, enthusiasts, students, and professionals support each other through blogs, YouTube videos, and forums. Because of this, LEGO® MINDSTORMS® robots are a great connected learning tool, perfect for learners on all levels to use and contribute to the community knowledge.

LEGO® MINDSTORMS® robots may be programmed to run autonomously or users may control them remotely using a variety of methods, such as a free app available for android and iOS devices. Since most robotics competitions require a mixture of autonomous and remote control functionality, the versatile LEGO® MINDSTORMS® brick is a common player in multiple levels of competition, from upper elementary school through college. New Rochelle Library Media Specialist Ryan Paulsen says that he is using RobotC on the LEGO® MINDSTORMS® brick with his FIRST Tech Challenge team, which serves as a sort of junior varsity team for the FIRST Robotics Competition team because, "it's fairly approachable and gets [students] thinking in the same way that [they'll] have to think in other programming languages."[10]

Of course, not all uses need be this advanced. In addition to stand-alone programs, camps, and clubs, Cuyahoga County Public Library has utilized LEGO® MINDSTORMS® robots in the Team Read-A-Book series, which aims to help elementary students who are struggling to improve their reading skills and to help their parents build advocacy and coaching skills. Students work with a librarian while parents work with a representative from the Learning Disabilities Association and then both groups come together for an enrichment activity. On the occasions when robotics is the activity, each parent partners with his or her child on a few basic challenges. The image-based programming environment combined with the open-ended problem solving, creativity, and critical thinking nature of the activities, provides a unique environment for students who may have one or more learning difficulties. Parents deeply enjoy the opportunity to see their children shine and view themselves as smart.

Like the LEGO® WeDo® kits, the LEGO® MINDSTORMS® kits may be augmented with additional LEGO® pieces. Building clubs using LEGO® bricks continue to attract library users throughout the nation, and enriching these programs with the power of motorized, programmable parts, provides a rich opportunity to build both STEAM and English Language Art skills. Students in the club might be challenged to create inventions to help literary characters out of their predicaments, or demonstrate the meaning of vocabulary words through dynamic builds.

Turnipseed also envisions LEGO® MINDSTORMS® as part of library makerspaces. Because the robots are made of LEGO® bricks, users can build, test, take apart, and rebuild. He points out that not only do kids love LEGO®, but also a vast community of adult enthusiasts create and connect online. As new adults emerge as digital natives, the combination of classic building blocks and technology may offer a perfect intergenerational blend to launch a creation space.

# VEX®

Just as LEGO® offers multiple robotics solutions, the VEX® fleet, produced by Innovation First International, Inc., includes products for each tier of learner. The three platforms include VEX® IQ, designed for elementary and middle school students, VEX® EDR, for those in middle school, high school, and beyond, and VEX® Pro, which is particularly geared for high-level competitions such as FIRST Robotics Competition. For the purposes of an introductory overview, only the VEX® IQ and VEX® EDR platforms will be discussed in the following section.

*How It Works:* As with LEGO® MINDSTORMS® robots, students build VEX® IQ robot bodies from plastic pieces that snap together without tools. Students may use provided instructions to build a standard model, or create their own. The VEX® IQ Robot Brain may be programmed to run autonomously or in conjunction with a manually operated controller. The Robot Brain includes a USB 2.0 port, a tether port for the controller, a radio port, and 12 Smart Ports for connecting motors and sensors. The VEX® website highlights three programming tools: Modkit, free graphical programming software, ROBOTC for VEX® IQ, and VEX® Assembler, a free 3-D Modeling software built on Autodesk 123D.

The VEX® EDR platform might be viewed as the traditional VEX® model. Students may build models from guides or create their own robot bodies using predrilled, metal components, nuts, and screws. The robot may be controlled using either the VEXnet Joystick, which resembles a typical gaming controller, and the VEX® Arm Cortex®-based Microcontroller. For autonomous programming, the VEX® website advertises ROBOTC for VEX®, EasyC for Cortex, and Flowol, a simple, graphical interface for young and new users.

*Age-Levels:* Innovation First International, Inc. markets VEX® IQ for elementary and middle school students aged eight and up, although a quick scan of forums reveals that like LEGO® MINDSTORMS®, older teen and adult hobbyists also enjoy the IQ platform. Innovation First International, Inc. identifies the VEX® EDR platform for "middle school, high school, and beyond."

*Costs:* It is challenging to pin down exact costs for VEX® products due to the number of customizable packages and individual parts offered, as well as the variety of potential uses, particularly for the VEX® EDR platform.

The VEX® IQ Super Kit retails for about $300 and includes all of the construction pieces needed for the basic Clawbot IQ build, as well as four smart motors, seven sensors, the Robot Brain, controller, and batteries. A classroom bundle that includes 12 Super Kits, for 24 students working in pairs, is about $3,500. Software options include the free Modkit and VEX® Assembler tools, and ROBOTC for VEX®, which sells from the VEX® website for about $80 for a single license, $300 for a six-seat license and $600 for a 30 seat license.

The VEX® EDR Super Kit retails for about $1,000 and includes all the materials needed to build the EDR Clawbot, nine sensors, three motors, and the VEXnet bundle that includes the joystick, microcontroller, and chargers. VEX® recommends one kit per two to six students. The Super Kit is designed for classroom and competition use, but those just getting started, or using the VEX® EDR in stand-alone classes may also consider purchasing the VEX® Clawbot Kit. The Clawbot Kit retails at about $150 and does not include a control system. The VEXnet Control system bundle including microcontroller and joystick sells for about $400. VEX® offers the same programming software options for VEX® EDR as VEX® IQ.

With either platform, the additional expense of computers should be considered. Those planning to participate in competitions will also need to budget for supplementary and replacement parts.

# Usage

Compared to the long-vetted LEGO® MINDSTORMS® system, the VEX® IQ platform is a relative newcomer to the scene of robotics products, having been launched as recently as 2013. Like LEGO® MINDSTORMS®, VEX® IQ is designed for class and competitive use, and the combination of snap together components with graphic programming software allows libraries to successfully host stand-alone introductory classes with minimal staff training. Unlike LEGO® MINDSTORMS®, the online community surrounding VEX® IQ is in its early stages; however, VEX® provides a free STEM curriculum designed for students in grades four through eight, which is made up of 12 units that may be used in sequence or as stand-alone classes. Though the VEX® IQ system targets students as young as eight, the ability to program with ROBOTC creates an opportunity to introduce and advance coding skills to all ages. With the ability to challenge participants with creative building, remote control driving, and coding, there are enough options available to support camps, clubs, and competition teams.

Since, like the VEX® IQ, the VEX® EDR platform can be manipulated without additional programming using the controller, it would certainly be possible for libraries to use VEX® EDR in stand-alone, introductory classes. The cost of the VEX® EDR platform may be better justified, however, by libraries planning to lead extensive classes, clubs, or camps using the extensive programming capabilities, or those intending to field a competition team. The VEX® competition webpage boasts that "more than 10,000 teams from 32 countries, participate in VEX® Robotics Competitions," so VEX® EDR is certainly a popular choice for this purpose. Public and Academic libraries looking to connect with new adults may wish to investigate the VEX® U competition for college-aged students. Though identification with a particular college or university is not required, this may be a good opportunity for institutions to partner.

# Money Matters

Ideally, a library would select the type of robots used by choosing that which best suits their educational goals and the class types that have been selected to reach them and then purchase the appropriate products. The abundance of donors interested in STEAM education may increase the possibility of this strategy and the scope to which libraries may dream, but even libraries starting out with the most modest of budgets may strategically plan for future growth. In this section, we'll explore possible sources of funding and tactical budgeting for any funds acquired.

# Finding Funding
## Small-Scale

The old adage "You have to spend money to make money" can apply to nonprofit institutions like libraries that are attempting to reassure potential funders that money will be used judiciously and effectively. A library that has invested the staff time and resources to host a pilot event or initiative and can demonstrate its value to the community of learners, stands a much better chance of receiving larger funding amounts from deep-pocketed funders. This may be a special event for Hour of Code, a LEGO® building club in which students take turns incorporating the library's single LEGO® WeDo® set, or a video of students interacting with a Sphero around the reference desk. These types of classes may not require a significant investment beyond time. Michael Cherry of Evansville Public Library recommends the free lesson plans available from PBS Kids' Design Squad website for easy to budget starter activities. Free technology literacy activities, many of which only require a computer or simply paper and pencil, are also available from the Code. org and the Computer Science Education Week websites among others. Successfully hosting these simple, stand-alone events may help inspire donors to further the cause.

Public libraries with money from friends groups or school libraries with discretionary funds may want to consider allocating a bit of money toward purchasing a starter robot. Heather Booth explains the shift that she's experienced through her work on the Robot Test Kitchen, "Thinking about spending money on robotics is no different than spending money on a program—like a magician, etc. . . . except that you can use the product again. You can purchase an expensive tech tool and still be a good steward." Bob Loftin agrees, and declares, "We have the best friends group in the world. Friends of the Plano Public Library System have been extremely helpful. They've been hugely supportive of robotics." Exemplifying how success breeds success, the Plano Public Library established an initial program using friends money and borrowing equipment from a local university, then applied for and received a grant to purchase 24 LEGO® MINDSTORMS® EV3 kits.

Of course, some libraries, already fiscally stretched, may need financial help to launch even a preliminary trial. Small-scale grants of $1,000 or less typically require minimal reporting and may be a good fit for librarians short on time and money. Before investigating the national resources listed below, libraries may want to check with local organizations and businesses that may offer mini grants or start-up funds limited to the region for which there may be less competition. Turnipseed reflects that he is always amazed by the support available for good plans, and he believes that libraries offer "a unique entrée to go out and talk to the business community," because business people may be intimidated or confused by what happens in a modern classroom, but they all think that they know what goes on in the library. Libraries focusing on 21st Century Skills are aligning with what businesses want to see in future workers, and Turnipseed encourages libraries to communicate this message to gain financial and technical support from local business.

*YALSA Teen Tech Week Grants:* Since 2013, the Young Adult Library Services Association division of the American Library Association has offered mini grants provided by Best Buy. In 2015, 20 mini grants of $1,000 were offered to support digital literacy classes in libraries during the annual Teen Tech Week event.

*Donors Choose.org:* School librarians working in U.S. public schools may post project requests on the site and members of the public can group fund the project.

*Dominion Mini Grants:* Public and private schools, and nonprofit organizations in geographic regions served by Dominion may apply for mini grants of up to $1,000, for "small projects that enhance the teaching of math and/or science."

*Foundation for Rural Service:* Those serving rural populations, may wish to apply for this annual grant. The program focus includes education and telecommunications, and awards may be $250 to $5,000.

## Full-Scale

As with small-scale funders, donors with deeper pockets may be more apt to fund libraries already demonstrating some success. Libraries might provide examples of how they have sparked interest with a single robot or small collection and detail plans for expansion. Kelly Czarnecki of Charlotte Mecklenburg Library's ImaginOn recommends investigating Google and Make Magazine's summer Maker Camp. Organizations may apply to receive reusable equipment, or they may simply employ the activity guides and videos provided online.

Those who are ready to dive in and purchase a robot fleet may need more extensive funds. Again, area businesses may be some of the most enthusiastic partners. Engineering firms, technology companies, industrial designers, and manufacturers often have a vested interest in growing and keeping local talent. Evansville Vanderburgh Public Library took full advantage of these types of local resources not only by joining Ivy Tech Community College's regional initiative, which provided the initial VEX® kit and professional development, but also by applying and receiving expansion funding from Toyota Manufacturing of Indiana, as well as the library's foundation and friends groups.

The national funders listed below represent only a few of the numerous supporters of STEM learning and literacy. Additional "rookie team" funding is typically available for those starting up competition teams and may be viewed on the particular competition's website.

*Dollar General Literacy Foundation:* Taking a holistic approach to literacy development, Dollar General's foundation offers grants for adult, families, and youth. Schools, public libraries, and nonprofit organizations may apply for a Youth Literacy Grant for up to $4,000 for initiatives that use technology to grow literacy.

*IMLS Sparks Ignition Grants:* The Institute of Museum and Library Services exist with the federal organization's National Leadership Grants for Libraries program and help libraries to initiate and evaluate new ideas. The awards range from $10,000 to $25,000.

*Motorola Solutions Foundation:* Innovation Generation (STEM) Local Impact Grants range between $15,000 and $60,000 and are intended for innovative, hands-on learning.

*American Honda Foundation:* The organization's funding priorities target youth STEM education, job training, and literacy, and awards range from $20,000 to $75,000. Applications are accepted quarterly.

# Budget Planning

Naturally, the scale of the initiative and the type of robots selected will determine the amount of money needed and how it should be spent. This section provides guidelines for three common scenarios. Note that shipping costs vary according to vendor and destination, so they are excluded from these estimates. Also, libraries that transport materials between locations or for outreach may need to budget in container and travel costs.

## Explorer Budget

Those just getting started may wish to experiment to see which type of robot product works best for their educational goals for the community. The Example Explorer Budget in Table 3.1 below would support, for instance, hosting a family night with stations for all ages.

**Table 3.1:** Example Explorer Budget

| Item | Price | Quantity | Extended Price |
|---|---|---|---|
| Cubelets Six Kit | $150 | 1 | $150 |
| LEGO® WeDo® Construction Set | $130 | 1 | $130 |
| LEGO® WeDo® Software | $90 | 1 | $90 |
| Sphero | $100 | 1 | $100 |
| Android Tablet for Sphero (such as Dell Venue) | $200 | 1 | $200 |
| Laptop for programming (such as Asus Transformer) | $300 | 1 | $300 |
| | | Total | $970 |

**Table 3.2:** Example Charter Budget

| Item | Price | Quantity | Extended Price |
|---|---|---|---|
| VEX® 6 Super Kits | $1,800 | 1 | $1,800 |
| ROBOTC for VEX® | | | |
| 6 seat license | $300 | 1 | $300 |
| Laptop for programming (such as Asus Transformer) | $300 | 5 | $1,500 |
| | | Total | $3,600 |

# Charter Budget

Those comfortable with technology, possessing some experience or healthy dose of confidence may be looking to get a robot set that could be used in stand-alone and series classes, clubs, or camps. The Example Charter Budget in Table 3.2 below assumes a class size of 12–24, with students working in teams of 2 to 3.

# Initiative Budget

Schools with multiple libraries or public libraries with multiple branches may be ready to implement robotics learning system-wide. The costs involved will depend on the number of locations and the willingness between all parties to share resources. The Example Initiative Budget in Table 3.3 assumes a class size of 12–24 students, with students working in teams of two to three. The 24 robots and laptops would break down into 4 sets of 6 kits each. Depending on the type of offerings and size of the library system, more or fewer sets may be needed. For the purposes of comparison, it may be worth considering that Cuyahoga County Public Library owns six such sets that rotate through the 27-branch

**Table 3.3:** Example Initiative Budget

| Item | Price | Quantity | Extended Price |
|---|---|---|---|
| LEGO® EV3 24 Core Sets and Site License | $4,367 | 1 | $4,367 |
| Laptop for programming (such as Asus Transformer) | $300 | 24 | $1,500 |
| Professional Development | $400 | 1 | $400 |
| | | Total | $6,267 |

system. This process is, however, expedited by central booking and shipping departments, and can get quite tight during summer camp season, so library systems without these support networks in place may wish to increase the ratio of equipment per location.

# CHAPTER 4

# Making the Case

Though the framework varies, every working school media specialist and public librarian in the nation is accountable to someone. Whether reporting to a school board, library board, director, manager, principal, or city council, librarians may need some language to convince others that a robotics program is a worthwhile investment and valuable tool. Funders, particularly of large-scale grants, also usually require some assurances that their investments are warranted.

## Outcome-Based Planning

Every major grant asks about desired outcomes or learning objectives and expects applicants to explain their strategies to reach them. Designing a learning experience from the goal down, not only prepares librarians to justify the project to administrators and potential funders, it also paves a pathway to success.

Conveniently, robotics learning supports a plethora of learning objectives common to school and public libraries, as discussed in Chapter 1. Additionally, individual school districts and public libraries may have strategic plans or annual goals that may be used. Some may view content standards and strategic plan points as limiting, but if we choose to view them as foundations and build our initiatives from their roots, it becomes much harder for dissenters to knock us down.

## Creating a Logic Model

Logic Models are used in a variety of professional settings to plan toward goals. When completing a logic model, planners use an "if this, then that" mentality to safeguard that the arguments to carry out the initiative are valid and the strategies to reach them sound. For instance, Mr. Jones the school librarian knows that students need to improve their research skills, so he spends some of his meager budget on quality databases, presents to relevant classes about them, and works his tail off creating pathfinders. How will he justify spending the money and time in this way rather than ordering class book sets and supervising study hall as some colleagues would prefer? How will he know if and when he's reached his goal? Creating logic models before embarking on such a project helps librarians make sure that they are investing their limited time and money in a way that will help students and demonstrate their value to stakeholders.

# Impact

As an example, let us follow the outcome-based planning of Mrs. Smith. She notices that a lot of students hang out in and around the library after school, and she knows that helping them find a constructive use of time is one of the ways the Search Institute's 2015 40 Developmental Assets for Adolescents list identifies that adults can help students grow up to be "healthy, caring, and responsible." She is also aware that a vast body of research, the main arguments of which are summarized well in Cullinan's 2000 report, reflects that students who read independently possess higher vocabulary, comprehension, and content knowledge across all areas, and do better on standardized tests than those who do not. She has also read about connected learning and thinks that libraries should help students build technology skills and a network of peers to help them continue to develop in their interests. Thinking about all of this, and her goals for the students, Mrs. Smith has identified the *impact*, or what the initiative will accomplish overall. She will use this impact statement, in Table 4.1, as the foundation for designing her initiative.

**Table 4.1:** Example Logic Model Impact Statement

IMPACT STATEMENT

Students drive inquiry and engage in learning during out-of-school time.

# Outcomes

She knows that to move forward she needs to integrate the project within her responsibilities as a librarian, convince her boss that the initiative is a good idea, and secure funding. To convince these three stakeholders, herself, her boss, and her funder, she needs to be able to explain what

**Table 4.2:** Example Logic Model Outcomes

IMPACT STATEMENT

Students drive inquiry and engage in learning during out-of-school time.

SHORT-TERM OUTCOMES

*Benefits for participants during and after activities*

| | | |
|---|---|---|
| The majority of participants will increase their reading for pleasure and for personal growth. | Most participants will improve how much they "read and comprehend complex literary and informational texts independently and proficiently." CCSS.ELA-LITERACY.CCRA.R.10 | Most participants will come to "exhibit a positive attitude toward using technology that supports collaboration, learning, and productivity." ISTE.DIGITALCITIZEN 5.B |

positive changes will happen because of this initiative. Now, she's thinking about *outcomes*, the measureable goals. One strategy might be to select at least one outcome desired by each stakeholder. For instance, part of her library's mission might be to promote literacy and reading, her boss might want everything to align to the common core, and a potential funder might be looking to grow technology literacy. The next step of her logic model, might, then, look something like Table 4.2.

In this example, Mrs. Smith has taken language from her library's strategic plan for her first outcome to ensure that her work supports the library's mission. The second outcome, from the Common Core State Standards English Language Arts Anchor Standards for Reading, addresses her boss's priorities. The third outcome, taken from the International Society of Technology in Education's standards for students, supports her funder's goals. It is crucial to note that Mrs. Smith selected outcomes that would move her toward the impact that she wants to have. She framed them in language that those she answers to hear well, but she made sure that she answered "yes" to the following question: If this outcome is reached, would it facilitate my goal of self-driven inquiry and engagement in out-of-school time learning?

# Activities

Next, Mrs. Smith thinks about the methods she will use to engage these students after-school and get them excited about reading and learning for pleasure and personal growth. Reflecting on her first outcome, "Participants will increase their reading for pleasure and for personal growth," she decides to make reading one of the activities. She thinks she could book talk a few new, enticing, high-quality fiction and nonfiction titles each session, and then create some sort of game using the robots that would encourage the students to explore the books for answers.

**Table 4.3:** Example Logic Model Activities

IMPACT STATEMENT

Students drive inquiry and engage in learning during out-of-school time

OUTCOMES

*Benefits for participants during and after activities*

| | | |
|---|---|---|
| The majority of participants will increase their reading for pleasure and for personal growth. | Most participants will improve how much they "read and comprehend complex literary and informational texts independently and proficiently." CCSS.ELA-LITERACY.CCRA.R.10 | Most participants will come to "exhibit a positive attitude toward using technology that supports collaboration, learning, and productivity." ISTE.DIGITALCITIZEN 5.B |

ACTIVITIES

*What the initiative does with the inputs to fulfill its mission*

"BookBOT Club"

- Use enticing, high-level fiction and nonfiction.
- Build and program robots to complete book-based challenges.
- Create online journal documenting discoveries about experiences including coding, engineering, and reading.

She'll have copies of the titles available for check out, so students who are hooked can continue reading on their own. She thinks these strategies will also help meet her second outcome, "Participants will read and comprehend complex literary and informational texts independently and proficiently," but to further meet it, she will also encourage students to research technical solutions and work together to understand and employ them. Lastly, as she thinks about her third outcome, she decides to have students work together to create a web journal about what they're doing, so they can "exhibit a positive attitude toward using technology that supports collaboration, learning, and productivity." These activities, based on the three outcomes, are compiled into the logic model as demonstrated in Table 4.3.

# Inputs

After double-checking to make sure that it seems likely that engaging students in her planned activities would lead to the types of changes she anticipates in her outcomes, Mrs. Smith thinks about what will be needed for the club. The *inputs*, or resources delivered to or consumed by the initiative, include any items that will be purchased and those that the library already supplies that support the activities. Including assumed resources such as staff time, library facilities and equipment, and library books, databases, and other materials on the logic model demonstrates to funders that the library is contributing to the project in-kind. This practice also helps planners make sure that they remember what to bring, reserve, or prepare and helps document the importance of library resources for stakeholders. In Table 4.4, the inputs are entered into the left hand column of the logic model to demonstrate how they will be inserted into, or feed the activities. Just as the outcomes determine the types of activities needed, so the activities determine the specific inputs required.

**Table 4.4:** Example Logic Model Inputs

IMPACT STATEMENT

Students drive inquiry and engage in learning during out-of-school time.

OUTCOMES

*Benefits for participants during and after activities*

| | | |
|---|---|---|
| The majority of participants will increase their reading for pleasure and for personal growth. | Most participants will improve how much they "read and comprehend complex literary and informational texts independently and proficiently." CCSS.ELA-LITERACY.CCRA.R.10 | Most participants will come to "exhibit a positive attitude toward using technology that supports collaboration, learning, and productivity." ISTE.DIGITALCITIZEN 5.B |

$\longrightarrow$

ACTIVITIES

*What the initiative does with the inputs to fulfill its mission*

INPUTS

*Resources delivered to or consumed by the initiative*

"BookBOT Club"

- staff time
- library books
- meeting room
- laptops and software
- robot kits
- game materials
- staff development
- high-speed Internet connection
- webhosting
- student time
- volunteer time

- Use enticing, high-level fiction and nonfiction
- Build and program robots to complete book-based challenges
- Create online journal documenting discoveries about experiences including coding, engineering, and reading

# Outputs

Many often confuse *outputs*, the direct products of initiative activities, with outcomes. Unlike outcomes, which examine the *why* of the initiative, outputs describe and count. To collect output data we ask, "how many, how much, which types." This information is important, and often libraries must regularly report outputs like circulation figures, door count statistics, hours of service, and numbers of class attendees. The outputs, however, do not tell the whole story or the intention.

Consider an initiative designed with an intended outcome to help youth in foster care find permanent placements. Over six months, the attendance numbers show a steady decrease. Reviewing these numbers alone might lead to a false assumption that the program is not working because fewer people are attending. However, placed within the context of the entire initiative, it may come to light that attendance is decreasing because the extent of permanent placements created through the initiative have significantly reduced the amount of youth still in foster care. Likewise, an initiative with the desired impact of increasing digital literacy may lead to a decrease in computer class attendance and in-branch computer use as participants become more skilled and purchase their own home computers.

Mrs. Smith knows, however, that some outputs can help document progress, and Table 4.5 reflects the type of outputs she expects from the activities. To measure how well she is advancing toward the outcome of increasing reading for pleasure and growth, she will need to do some pre- and post data collection. How many books are participants independently reading before joining the club, and how many are they independently reading after? The output of the number of books checked out by participants may help illuminate this question.

Mrs. Smith may also be able to use outputs such as videos of students collaborating, pictures of robots built, and numbers of enthusiastic community responses on the website to create a report for her stakeholders and create enthusiasm around her initiative. Her boss might free up her schedule to expand the club, the funder might invite her to apply for another grant, and her colleagues may look for new ways to collaborate with her.

# Indicators

Mrs. Smith reviews her logic model so far and feels confident that it is reasonable to assume that the activities she has planned will be achievable with the inputs that she has identified and will accomplish the outcomes and overall impact that she desires. Her next step is to prepare

**Table 4.5:** Example Logic Model Outputs

IMPACT STATEMENT

Students drive inquiry and engage in learning during out-of-school time.

OUTCOMES

*Benefits for participants during and after activities*

| | | |
|---|---|---|
| The majority of participants will increase their reading for pleasure and for personal growth. | Most participants will improve how much they "read and comprehend complex literary and informational texts independently and proficiently." CCSS.ELA-LITERACY.CCRA.R.10 | Most participants will come to "exhibit a positive attitude toward using technology that supports collaboration, learning, and productivity." ISTE.DIGITALCITIZEN 5.B |

ACTIVITIES

*What the initiative does with the inputs to fulfill its mission*

| → | | → |
|---|---|---|
| INPUTS | "BookBOT Club" | OUTPUTS |
| *Resources delivered to or consumed by the initiative* | | *The direct products of initiative activities* |
| • staff time <br> • library books <br> • meeting room <br> • laptops and software <br> • robot kits <br> • game materials <br> • staff development <br> • high-speed Internet connection <br> • webhosting <br> • student time <br> • volunteer time | • Use enticing, high-level fiction and nonfiction <br> • Build and program robots to complete book-based challenges <br> • Create online journal documenting discoveries about experiences including coding, engineering, and reading | • # of sessions <br> • # of books checked out by participants <br> • types of robots created <br> • creative solutions reached <br> • photos and videos of students in action <br> • the web journal <br> • # of volunteer hours <br> • # of page hits and comments <br> • # of attendees |

to prove her theory. *Indicators* provide evidence that a certain result has or has not been achieved, or that an initiative has had the intended effect. This is why the outcome statements are worded as measurable statements; they can be true or false. If Mrs. Smith can show that more than 50 percent of participants did, in fact "increase their reading for pleasure and for personal growth," during and after their time in the club she has created a strong case that her methods are effective. By identifying her indicators prior to the initiative's start, Mrs. Smith makes it easier to do pre- and post assessment. For instance, at the beginning of the club she might poll students about the number of books they typically read per week during the school year and then repeat the process after several sessions of the club.

An increase might lead Mrs. Smith to assume that the club is having the desired effect; however, it is important to remember that correlation does not equal causation. The students may be reading more for pleasure because the newest book in a popular series came out during the quarter, or because a local radio station is giving away concert tickets to the student who reads the most books about a visiting celebrity, or any number of other factors. So, Mrs. Smith adds to the poll, asking students who are reading more to self-report why they are reading the amount that they are reading. If 65 percent of students are reading more, and 51 percent of them say that it is because of their experiences in the club, then Mrs. Smith can more accurately assume that she has reached that outcome. Moving forward, she may want to increase her goal from "the majority of participants" to, say, "65 percent of participants." She may also want to investigate why some students aren't reading more. Is it because they were already reading as much as possible in their free time? Do they prefer genres that have not been discussed? These types of questions wouldn't be indicators for the purposes of outcome measurement, but they could be good research tools to help Mrs. Smith improve the initiative.

Choosing the best indicators can be challenging. Just as when selecting outcomes, it is important to narrow the focus to only those the initiative will impact. If Mrs. Smith had set her outcome to increase how much *all* of the students in a certain grade-level were reading, she would need to plan her activities and assessment to include every single student, but since she limited her intended impact to only those participating in the club, it is only necessary and appropriate to gather data about this smaller population's reading habits.

It may be simplest to begin by phrasing indicators as questions. These may be written as survey questions for the participant or as guiding research questions for the project planner. Though some of these questions may be monitoring student progress, it is important to remember that the point is to assess the initiative, not the students. Some guidelines for creating indicators are:

*How accurately does this indicator reflect outcome achievement?*
Mrs. Smith may be able to use the data she collects about how much and why students are reading to partially answer the second outcome, "Most participants will improve how much they 'read and comprehend complex literary and informational texts independently and proficiently'," but that data does not speak to how well students are comprehending what they read. She will need to find another way to evaluate how well the project is helping students to improve comprehension.

*Will there be data to answer this indicator? Is it quantifiable?* This can be frustrating because some very worthy outcomes may not have readily available or realistically collectable data. For instance, to fully gauge how well the BookBOT Club activities are helping to improve comprehension, Mrs. Smith would need to isolate participants from any other factors that could improve comprehension and pre- and posttest them. This is not realistic for many reasons. Comprehension levels would, in any case, be difficult to quantify without extensive testing. Since this is a voluntary after-school club, Mrs. Smith feels that this level of testing would be counterproductive to creating enthusiasm for reading and learning and wouldn't really be an accurate indicator anyway. She knows that quantifiable data speaks well to stakeholders though, so she adds a question to the pre- and postsurvey for students to self-report their comprehension levels. She worries, however, that the students' answers may not accurately reflect the whole picture, so she also makes sure to gather qualitative data, like examples of students' "aha moments," images of students referring to complex texts while problem solving, and related anecdotes from students and volunteers. Though it's best to gather some quantifiable data, if at all possible, qualitative information can help to provide necessary context to interpret what's happening and flesh out the indicator.

## Using the Logic Model

Even if a funder or supervisor does not require a completed logic model, the process of creating one expedites grant writing and provides a firm foundation for librarians to anticipate questions and potential problems. For long-term projects, facilitators can take periodic measurements using the indicators and often make simple changes to improve the activities, clarify outcomes, or adjust indicators. Doing this work up front also prepares librarians to sing their successes. After completion of an effective initiative, it is easy to pull together a presentation using the outcomes as section guides, and the indicators and outputs as examples. Those in authority are quite likely to endorse future projects of those who have already demonstrated their aptitude for achievement.

Logic models are also great tools for creating transparency and collaboration between all stakeholders. They may be posted on initiative websites to enable potential sponsors to ask intelligent questions and defend their investment. Students involved in the initiative might point out fallacies or potential opportunities. A logic model is a great tool to have on hand when someone asks, "Why are we doing this?"

Each ensuing chapter follows this practice and begins with a full logic model to describe the goals of the activities within. Though scaled to different levels, each activity guide, whether for a stand-alone, camp, or club initiative, begins with the desired outcomes as its foundation. As evidenced in the next chapter, even a one-day, one-time event may have a lasting impact when planned accordingly.

# CHAPTER 5

# Stand-Alone
# Activity Guide

The activities in this chapter are designed to be experienced at a one-day, one-time event. The Appendix provides the link for numerous downloadable, printable resources such as the logic model, activity sheets, outcome measurement tools, and videos and building guides of possible solutions. The activities may be completed with a wide variety of educational robotics products, and the capabilities required are listed in the details of each challenge.

## Preparation and Structure

When planning a stand-alone event, facilitators and hosting libraries should consider the intended clientele spectrum, the learning goals, and supporting components such as time, space, and materials needed. In the next section, we review these factors and how they may be adapted to suit particular scenarios.

## Outcomes

Because this is a single-day event, opportunities are limited to observe and measure the impact or change felt by participants, so the Robot Jungle Logic Model in Table 5.1 lists only two outcomes and both are fairly open.

1.  Most participants will increase ability to understand and creatively interpret literature.

2.  Most participants will discover and explore new areas of interest.

**Table 5.1:** Robot Jungle Logic Model

IMPACT STATEMENT

Community engaged in lifelong learning

OUTCOMES

*Benefits for participants during and after activities*

| | |
|---|---|
| Most participants will increase ability to understand and creatively interpret texts. CCSS.ELA-LITERACY. CCRA.R.3, R.4 & L.4 | Most participants will discover and explore new areas of interest. |
| | CCSS.ELA-LITERACY.CCRA.R.10 |
| AASL 1.1.6 & 4.1.3 | AASL 1.2.1. 4.3.3 & 4.4.1 |
| ISTE 1B, 1C & 2D | ISTE 4A & 5C |

| INPUTS | ACTIVITIES | OUTPUTS |
|---|---|---|
| | *What the initiative does with the inputs to fulfill its mission* | |
| → | | → |
| | "Robot Jungle" | |
| *Resources delivered to or consumed by the initiative* | | *The direct products of initiative activities* |
| • staff time | • Interpret events in the story | • # of attendees |
| • physical space, tables and chairs | • Build simple robots using basic mechanical concepts and story themes | • # of event hours |
| • robot sets | | • list of words explored |
| • staff development | | • photos of creative solutions |
| • volunteers | • Explore discovered interests independently | • photos and videos of participants in action |
| • laptops and Internet | | • # of creative solutions reached |
| • library books | | • # of volunteers and volunteer hours |
| • consumable materials (paper, pens, etc.) | | • circulation of books and use of library resources |

The activities are designed to address specific **+**CCSS-ELA Anchor Standards, ❖ISTE Technology Standards, and the ⊘AASL Standards for the 21st Century Learner as indicated on the logic model and listed in Table 5.2; however, there are many other standards being addressed and which facilitators may choose to develop further.

## *Type of Event*

There are two types of stand-alone events for which these activities are specifically designed. The first is a larger open house model that routes participants through stations, and the second option is more of a traditional though active class. Tips for both the *stations* and *class* models are provided throughout. Each station is made up of one challenge.

**Table 5.2:** Robot Jungle Standards

IMPACT STATEMENT

Community engaged in Lifelong Learning

OUTCOMES

| | |
|---|---|
| Most participants will increase ability to understand and creatively interpret texts. | Most participants discover and explore new areas of interest. |

STANDARDS

| | |
|---|---|
| CCSS.ELA-LITERACY.CCRA.R.3<br>Analyze how and why individuals, events, or ideas develop and interact over the course of a text. | CCSS.ELA-LITERACY.CCRA.R.10<br>Read and comprehend complex literary and informational texts independently and proficiently. |
| CCSS.ELA-LITERACY.CCRA.R.4<br>Interpret words and phrases as they are used in a text, including determining technical, connotative, and figurative meanings, and analyze how specific word choices shape meaning or tone. | |
| CCSS.ELA-LITERACY.CCRA.L.6<br>Acquire and use accurately a range of general academic and domain-specific words and phrases sufficient for reading, writing, speaking, and listening at the college and career readiness level; demonstrate independence in gathering vocabulary knowledge when encountering an unknown term important to comprehension or expression. | |
| AASL 1.1.6 Read, view, and listen for information presented in any format (e.g., textual, visual, media, digital) in order to make inferences and gather meaning. | AASL 1.2.1 Display initiative and engagement by posing questions and investigating the answers beyond the collection of superficial facts. |
| AASL 4.1.3 Respond to literature and creative expressions of ideas in various formats and genres. | AASL 4.3.3 Seek opportunities for pursuing personal and aesthetic growth. |
| | AASL 4.4.1 Identify own areas of interest. |
| ISTE 1B Create original works as a means of personal or group expression. | ISTE 4A Identify and define authentic problems and significant questions for investigation. |
| ISTE 1C Use models and simulations to explore complex systems and issues. | ISTE 5C Demonstrate personal responsibility for lifelong learning. |
| ISTE 2D Contribute to project teams to produce original works or solve problems. | |

INDICATORS

| | |
|---|---|
| Observation and postsurvey. | Observation and postsurvey. |

# *Publicity Description*

Below are two example publicity descriptions that may be adapted to suit a library's particular needs:

*Robot Jungle Adventure (Stations):* Whether young in years or young at heart, learners of all ages can explore programming, build animatronic creatures, and bring Rudyard Kipling's classic stories from *The Jungle*

*Book* to life with our educational robots. Guided tours leave at 2 P.M., 2:30 P.M., and 3:00 P.M. Book your passage early.

*Robot Jungle School (Class):* Wild about making stuff? Build and program simple robots in this class for ages (x) to (x). We'll build animatronic creatures and bring Rudyard Kipling's classic stories from *The Jungle Book* to life with our educational robots. Space is limited, so register early!

# Time Allotment

Participants should be allotted about 30 minutes for each challenge, although facilitators who are incorporating all extension activities may plan for more time. The publicity description above for the stations model assumes that three different groups will rotate through four stations. If the groups stagger their start times every 30 minutes, the entire event would be 3 hours. Stand-alone classes are typically one to two hours, though older students may be able to stay engaged longer if instructors wish to extend the activities. In class settings, it is common not to complete all challenges. Instructors may choose two to target. Those concerned about meeting the outcomes on the logic model will want to make sure to include Challenge 4.

# Age-Levels

These activities may be adapted for any combination in the 8–24-year-old range. The stations model can truly serve all ages; however, keep in mind that events advertised for families typically attract adults with children. Those intending to target new adults without children may wish to skew the description accordingly.

Classes typically target a more defined age bracket, as participants will be working collaboratively and in closer proximity. The younger the participants, the more significant the developmental differences between age levels become. A 20-year-old and a 24-year-old may easily work well together, whereas an 8-year-old and 12-year-old may struggle to socialize well and collaborate on equal footing. Typically, it is best to keep the age difference less than 2 years apart for those 12 and younger, 3 years apart for those aged 13 to 18, and up to 5 years for those between 19 and 24 years old.

# Class Size

One of the benefits of stand-alone events is that libraries may offer multiple iterations of the same class in the same time it might take to lead a camp or series. For instance, instead of the same 12 students attending a 4-day, 2-hour-a-day camp, 4 groups of 12 students each could attend 4 different offerings of the same class, so that 48 students would benefit from the experience. Because of this benefit, it is possible to keep class sizes small and still reach a larger number of community members. Keeping student to instructor ratios around 12 or below is necessary to enable more personalized and creative learning.

Stations may reach larger numbers of people depending on the number of facilitators, the amount of equipment available, the extent to which challenges are truncated, and the total length of the event. For example, if 4 facilitators run groups of 12 that are staggered every 30 minutes through 4 stations, 60 participants will be engaged in a 4-hour event, or 15 customers per hour. Of course, because the pace and atmosphere of such an event is typically hectic, the amount of deep learning and personalized connections may be lower. When considering class sizes, consider that only two to three participants should share a robot at any given station.

# Robots

These activities are particularly suited to LEGO® WeDo®; however, with the exception of Bee-Bot, any of the robots presented in Chapter 3 may be used effectively. Challenge adaptations for certain robot models are provided when necessary. Those using LEGO® MINDSTORMS® or VEX® robots will want to prebuild a basic model for students to modify, or dedicate an hour of class time to building a robot.

# Supplies and Other Equipment

Beyond robots, there are few additional items needed for these activities. One computer or tablet per team will be necessary for those using robots that require them for programming, but those leading a station event will need additional online stations for research in Station 4 as well as relevant books, the particulars of which will be discussed more in depth in the challenge description. Activities in Challenge 1 require a blindfold, a shoebox, and a small ball, such as a table tennis or golf ball.

Facilitators may choose to print a Jungle Map, available for download, for each student or team to keep track of progress through the challenges. For younger students in particular, it is recommended that a relevant sticker or stamp be available for each challenge. For instance, Challenge 1 involves wolves primarily, Challenge 2 involves tiger, and Challenge 3 involves snakes and monkeys. So each time a student completes a challenge the relevant animal stamp or sticker may be awarded on his Jungle Map. The Jungle Map is simply a tool, however, and is not necessary to complete the challenges.

Some optional props for challenges include:

- Small baby or wolf figurines
- Small red item representing fire—for those using LEGO® WeDo®, LEGO® wands with a red brick attached work well

# Guide Components

The guide includes similar elements for each challenge, including some preparatory technical studies, a read aloud selection, a description of the challenge, programming considerations, and an example solution.

## *Learn Together*

Stand-alone events are intended to be introductory in nature, so each challenge begins with a preliminary activity to acquaint participants with some basic concepts of machines and mechanisms that may help with the upcoming challenge. It is expected that the instructor will have acquainted herself with the basic operations of the robot being used and will be able to coach students through processes necessary to complete the challenges.

## *Traditional Literacy*

Robot Jungle challenges are based on events in Rudyard Kipling's classic *The Jungle Book*. The stories of *The Jungle Book* were originally published individually in magazines. The rights to the stories themselves and the collection of them known as *The Jungle Book* have passed into the public domain. There are, however, numerous versions of *The Jungle Book* published in print form that retain some manner of copyright, whether for the illustrations, typesetting, or abridgement/rendition. A recent edition of the full, unabridged text that libraries may already have in their collections or wish to purchase is the 2012 Random House issue, with a forward by Neil Gaiman and illustrations by John Lockwood Kipling. Free to use copies of the original text are available to print and read in browser from World Book Online Reference Center. Project Gutenberg also offers the original text to be read online and on devices that accept ePub and Kindle editions.

Though reading aloud to participants can help participants comprehend texts at higher reading levels than their own, the original text language may still prove a bit challenging for some participants as MetaMetrics rates it at an 1100 Lexile level. Those working with younger students may wish to investigate an abridged version such as the 2014 offering from Cider Mill Press, illustrated by Don Daily and truncated by Elizabeth Encarnacion. This picture book version includes condensed versions of all of the stories used in the challenges.

## Read Together

Before the announcement of each challenge, participants will discover its root in the text by reading the appropriate section. Instructors may read aloud themselves, play from an audiobook recording, or ask for student volunteers. Evade hurt feelings and embarrassment by eschewing "round reading" or mandatory reading aloud. If possible, provide enough copies for all to follow along in the text, so students can see unfamiliar words in action. This reading time serves not only as research for the challenges, but also as a commercial for the featured book and the joy of reading. It is common for students to want to read the book in its entirety either at the event or at home. Instructors are encouraged to provide copies for checkout.

## Vocabulary

Vocabulary words that are introduced in each Challenge are defined from *Merriam-Webster's Collegiate Dictionary*, 11th Edition. To build comprehension, however, instructors are encouraged to discuss and define the words as a group from contextual learning. The vocabulary words are selected either from the book or from relevant technology concepts. Instructors may certainly replace or augment the example vocabulary words provided with ones more suited to a particular age group, robot product, or extension activity.

## *Challenge Brief*

The challenge brief provides language to announce the challenge and any pertinent rules, restrictions, or clarifications; however, all challenges are intentionally left open to interpretation to maximize creative thinking and the opportunity for multiple correct solutions. Instructors are also encouraged to adapt the challenges to the needs of the students, the capabilities of the robot, or the class environment.

## *One Possible Solution*

An example programming solution to each challenge is included to provide some insight to instructors as they coach students. Videos of the solutions in action and building guides for the custom models used in the videos are available from the website listed in the Appendix. Instructors may be tempted to construct a similar model for class demonstration; however, this can lead to copying of the model rather than creative and critical thinking and problem solving. All solutions provided use LEGO® WeDo® kits and software.

# Challenge 1: Raising Mowgli

In the first challenge, participants are introduced to baby Mowgli as he enters the jungle and to the three common attributes of a robot. For the activities in this section a blindfold, a box, and a small ball, like a table tennis ball are needed. This challenge focuses on the robot's sensors and brain, so only those programming elements that deal with sensors need be introduced.

## *Learn Together*

Every existing robot is a *machine*, or a *device that transmits force to perform a specific task*, but not every machine is a robot. Robots are different from machines, but similar to people, because they must be able to take in information, think about it, and react.

## Come to Your Senses Activity ✪AASL 1.1.6

Blindfold one student, and lead her away from the group. Ask the student if she thinks the rest of the group is in front of her or behind her. Is she nearer to the door or farther? Remove the blindfold. As a group, discuss what senses the student used to determine her orientation to the world around her.

## A Swiftly Tilting Robot ❖ ISTE 1C

Some robots use tilt sensors to better understand how they are oriented in the world. Discuss as a group "How do you think the tilt sensor 'knows' when it is this way, that way, or not tilted?"

Place the ball inside an empty box. Gently tilt the model this way, that way, up and down. Ask students, "What happens to the ball inside?"

Rolling-ball type tilt sensors are similarly structured. When the ball, made of a conductive material touches the walls of the cavity, which are poles, it shorts them, effectively acting as a switch throw. The robot's programming interprets this *input* to know which direction the sensor has tilted along an *axis*.

## Vocabulary

✚CCSS.ELA-LITERACY.CCRA.R.4 & L.6 Based on the previous discussion, ask the group to define these terms in their own words:

*axis*—(noun) *a real or imaginary line around which an object may rotate*
*input*—(noun) *information entered into a microprocessor or computer*

## Programming 101

Coach students in the basic controls of the robot that are relevant to the challenge. For instance, if using LEGO® WeDo® products, demonstrate how the tilt sensor's settings may be adjusted in the software.

## *Read Together*

Read "Mowgli's Brothers" from beginning through, "and that is how Mowgli was entered into the Seeonee Wolf Pack for the price of a bull and on Baloo's good word." In the abbreviated version by Daily, "Mowgli's Brothers" ends at this point.

## *Challenge Brief*

Like Shere Khan, react when the wolves *raise* the baby.

✚CCSS.ELA-LITERACY.CCRA.R.4 Language is "punny"! As a group, define the word *raise*. What are two possible definitions? 1. To lift up. 2. To bring to maturity, to rear (as a child). Why might the challenge brief be a pun?

## *One Possible Solution* ✪*AASL 4.1.3* ❖*ISTE 1B & 2D*

The example build for this solution is a simple box (representing a crèche) made of LEGO® bricks in which the baby figurine lies. Attached to the box is the tilt sensor. The model instructions can be viewed, in action with the program in a video from the website listed in the Appendix.

**Figure 5.1:** Raising Mowgli Possible Program

In the example shown in Figure 5.1, the first block after the play button is the Display Block, which uses the computer screen to display background #5, which represents the jungle into which Mowgli crawled. In the next block, the tilt sensor input is set to wait to continue on in the program until the sensor picks up movement in any direction. When the crèche with the baby is raised, this movement triggers the next Display Block to move to background #9, a cave, representing the wolf family's lair. The Sound Block at the end triggers sound #14, a roar for Shere Khan's rage.

Those using Sphero may adapt the challenge so that the Sphero displays a color change when picked up, triggered by the built in accelerometer. Cubelets might react by flashing when the baby is raised from in front of a light sensor where it was blocking the light. VEX® and LEGO® MINDSTORMS® robots have a variety of sensors that will work to trigger a reaction. Encourage students to be creative in considering what a reaction might be.

## Challenge 2: The Red Flower

In the second challenge, Mowgli must use his brains and his body to ward off the threats of his brothers and Shere Khan, and students learn about components that make up robots' bodies.

## *Learn Together*

In the previous challenge, we explored how robots use sensors to take in information about the world around them. Once robots take in and process information, they need to react. To react physically, a robot needs a body. Like cars, robot bodies may use motors, axles, and gears.

# Programming 101 ✚CCSS.ELA-LITERACY.CCRA.L.6
✪AASL 1.1.6 ❖ISTE 1C

With LEGO® WeDo®, LEGO® MINDSTORMS®, or VEX® robots show students how to program a gear to spin on an axle, first clockwise, then counterclockwise. If time allows, experiment with attaching a secondary or follower gear. Notice that the teeth of the lead gear drive the follower gear in the opposite direction.

If using Cubelets or Sphero, have students research the internal components of each. For those using LEGO® WeDo®, introduction of crown gears may also be helpful for this challenge. For all robots, ask students to identify the motor(s), gear(s), and axle(s) in use.

## *Vocabulary*

*motor*—(noun) *a machine that converts electrical energy into (typically rotating) mechanical energy*

*axle*—(noun) *a rod around which an object, such as a wheel, may rotate*

*gear*—(noun) *a wheel that may transfer energy to another gear through meshed "teeth"*

*clockwise*—(adjective) *in the same direction as the hands of a clock*

*counterclockwise*—(adjective) *in the opposite direction of the hands of a clock*

## *Read Together*

Read the second section of "Mowgli's Brothers" from, "Now you must be content to skip ten or eleven whole years| . . .|" through to the end. In the abbreviated Daily version, "The Red Flower" is separated into its own story.

✚CCSS.ELA-LITERACY.CCRA.R.3 ✪AASL 1.1.6

Ask students, "Why do you think Mowgli's adopted wolf brothers turn on him?" Some possible responses include:

- They are jealous of the special attention he receives.
- Shere Khan has influenced them with negative thoughts.
- Because they are afraid of someone who is different.

Ask students, "Why are the animals afraid of *the red flower*, fire, and Mowgli is not?" Some possible responses include:

- Mowgli remembers being warm and safe near a fireplace when he was a baby.

- As a human, Mowgli has different instincts than the animals.

- Mowgli knows how to control the fire, and the animals do not.

## Challenge Brief

Wave a torch to scare off Shere Khan and the young wolves.

## One Possible Solution

⊙AASL 4.1.3 ❖ISTE 1B & 2D

In the example shown in Figure 5.3, the LEGO® figurine, representing Mowgli, holds a torch made from a LEGO® wand piece and a red bead,

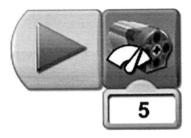

**Figure 5.2:** The Red Flower Possible Program

**Figure 5.3:** The Red Flower Possible Build

and stands atop a brick that turns when the axle turns. The axle turns from the rotation of a crown gear. The crown gear's teeth are intermeshed with that of a follower gear, which is connected to the lead gear coming off the axle from the motor. As indicated in Figure 5.2, the program simply turns the motor clockwise at 50 percent power.

Those using Sphero might program it to turn red and spin in widening circles. Cubelets might flash a warning in a circle. LEGO® MINDSTORMS® and VEX® robot users might add a rotating arm.

# Challenge 3: Kaa's Hunting

This third challenge provides opportunities for students to be truly creative in both building and programming. This challenge has two Read Together portions to break up the story and provide context.

## *Read Together*

Read from the beginning of "Kaa's Hunting" until Mowgli has been taken to the Cold Lairs and wonders, "Do they never go to sleep? Now there is a cloud coming to cover that moon. If it were only a big enough cloud I might try to run away in the darkness. But I am tired."

## Guiding Questions for Discussion ✚CCSS. ELALITERACY. CCRA.R.3 ✪AASL 1.1.6 & 4.1.3

When the story starts, Baloo is teaching Mowgli how to speak to different animals. Ask students, "If you could speak the language of any animal, which would you choose and why?"

Ask Students, "Why is it important for Mowgli to be able to speak the Master Words for each jungle animal?" Some possible responses include:

- The Master Words act as a password to allow passage through that animal's hunting grounds.

- The Master Words encourage other animals to view Mowgli as friendly.

- The Master Words can be used to ask another animal for help.

## Compare and Contrast

Watch the music video of "I Wanna Be Like You" posted on YouTube by Disney Movies Anywhere®. Ask students, "How do the primates in the video differ from the monkeys in the book?" Some possible responses include:

- There is no monkey king in the book.

- King Louie is an Orangutan, whereas the monkeys are described as gray apes.

- The monkeys in the book want Mowgli to teach them how to build houses, whereas the monkeys in the video want Mowgli to tell them how to make fire.

## Learn Together

This challenge presents an opportunity to learn about pulleys and belts, which are included in LEGO® WeDo®, EV3, and VEX® IQ sets. Those using robots without pulleys and belts might skip this section or replace it with terms that make sense to the robots employed.

### Programming 101 ✚CCSS.ELA-LITERACY.CCRA.L.6 ✪AASL 1.1.6 ❖ISTE 1C

Show students how to connect two pulleys with a belt, and program and power movement. Note that two pulleys connected by a single loop of the same belt move in the same direction as each other, whereas an even number of gears that are connected turn in opposite directions from one another. When a twist is placed in the belt, however, the pulleys turn in opposite directions.

### Vocabulary

*pulley*— (noun) *a wheel that transfers energy through a belt that rotates around its indented edge*
*belt*—(noun) *a strip of malleable material that connects to itself around at least one pulley*

## Read Together

Summarize what has happened in "Kaa's Hunting" so far, then pick up from "That same cloud was being watched by two good friends in the ruined ditch below the city wall| ...|" through to the end of the story.

# Challenge Brief

Save Mowgli from the pesky primates! Communicate to Rann, and then hypnotize the monkeys.

# One Possible Solution

✪AASL 4.1.3 ❖ISTE 1B & 2D

In this example, the program in Figure 5.4 uses two Sound Blocks to get Rann's attention by first whistling then playing a bird sound effect. The third block simple turns on the motor at 40 percent power. The custom build in Figure 5.5 is meant to look like a snake's head, with the pulleys representing the eyes.

**Figure 5.4:** Kaa's Hunting Possible Program

**Figure 5.5:** Kaa's Hunting Possible Build

Those using Sphero might have students create hypnotizing patterns, or change the challenge to a choreographed dance to the King Louie music.

Students using Cubelets might use the speaker to signal for Rann and then send the robot in circles.

With LEGO® MINDSTORMS® and VEX®, the possibilities are endless, but could include a combination of dance and hypnotizing motion.

# Challenge 4: Choose Your Own Path

Several times throughout *The Jungle Book*, Mowgli must choose his own path. In this challenge, each student will pick his own. This is an opportunity for students to delve more deeply into topics skimmed in earlier challenges. Students may choose from one of the inspirational questions below, or identify and define an original question for investigation. The question may involve researching with databases, reading books from the library's collection, or connecting with the online coding community. Students may work with partners or small teams if they choose, or they may work independently.

✚CCSS.ELA-LITERACY.CCRA.R.10 ✪AASL 1.2.1, 4.1.3 4.3.3, 4.4.1 ❖ISTE 4A, 1B & 5C

In "Kaa's Hunting" the great snake puts the monkeys into a trance before devouring them. Research Indian rock pythons. How big can they get? Can they really hypnotize prey? Do they eat monkeys? How could your robot mimic some of Kaa's characteristics?

✚CCSS.ELA-LITERACY.CCRA.R.10 ✪AASL 1.2.1, 4.1.3 4.3.3, 4.4.1 ❖ISTE 4A, 1B & 5C

In *The Jungle Book*, Bagheera is said to be a black panther. See what you can find out about black panthers in India. How could your robot mimic some of Bagheera's characteristics?

✚CCSS.ELA-LITERACY.CCRA.R.10 ✪AASL 4.1.3 ❖ISTE 1B & 2D

In the English language, we sometimes say that someone was "raised by wolves" if the person is uncouth or lacking manners. When Mowgli comes to the wolf pack as a baby, Father Wolf says that he has heard of human children being raised by wolves from time to time. See what examples you can find, whether legends or documented cases, and compare them.

✚CCSS.ELA-LITERACY.CCRA.R.10 ✪AASL 1.2.1, 4.1.3 4.3.3, 4.4.1
❖ISTE 4A, 1B & 5C

For those in the jungle, hunting and tracking are vital skills for survival. Research some ways that animals and humans track. How could you make a robot that tracks its prey?

In this chapter, we explored how we could introduce students to basic STEAM concepts while supporting traditional literacy development through analyzation of fiction and nonfiction texts. The stated outcomes for these activities were more about discovery and creating enthusiasm than about deep learning. The next chapter provides a blueprint for engaging eager learners in more advanced challenges in a multisession camp.

# CHAPTER 6

# Camp Activity Guide

The activities in this chapter are designed to be experienced over several sessions, such as multiple class periods, an afterschool mini series or a week-long camp. For the sake of brevity, the term *camp* is used throughout. Individual camp challenges may, however, also be used in stand-alone classes, clubs, or other settings.

The Appendix provides the link for numerous downloadable, printable resources such as the game board, activity sheets, outcome measurement tools, and videos and building guides of possible solutions. The challenges may be completed with a wide variety of educational robotics products, and the capabilities required are listed in the details of each challenge.

## Preparation and Structure

Prior to the first day of camp, certain elements need to be considered by the facilitator and hosting library. These elements include the learning objectives or desired outcomes for those attending camp, the target audience, and the type of equipment and materials needed.

## Outcomes

The activities in the camp are rooted from the ✚CCSS-ELA Anchor Standards, ❖ISTE Technology Standards, and the ◎AASL Standards for the 21st Century Learner, so there are numerous potential opportunities for participants to build both traditional and technology literacy. The specific outcomes and standards identified on the logic model (Table 6.1) and indicator table (Table 6.2) were particularly targeted in the design, and may be some of the most readily quantifiable. Facilitators may, however, tweak the camp activities and logic model to emphasize other standards as suits local need. The three main outcomes for Follow the White RabBOT Camp are:

1. Most participants will gain technological knowledge, skills, and abilities.
2. Most participants will augment technical and linguistic vocabulary.
3. Most participants will become more comfortable and adept at communicating and collaborating with peers.

**Table 6.1:** Follow the White RabBOT Camp Logic Model

IMPACT STATEMENT

Students rich in traditional and digital literacy

OUTCOMES

*Benefits for participants during and after activities*

| Most participants will gain technological knowledge, skills, and abilities. | Most participants will augment technical and linguistic vocabulary. | Most participants will become more comfortable and adept at communicating and collaborating with peers. |
|---|---|---|
| AASL 1.1.2, 1.1.8 | CCSS.ELA-LITERACY.CCRA.L.4 AASL 1.1.4 & 1.1.6 | CCSS.ELA-LITERACY.CCRA.SL.1 |
| ISTE 6A & 6D | | AASL 1.1.9, 2.1.5, 3.1.2, & 3.2.3 |
| | | ISTE 2D & 5B |

| | ACTIVITIES | |
|---|---|---|
| | *What the initiative does with the inputs to fulfill its mission* | |
| → | "White RabBOT Camp" | → |
| INPUTS | | OUTPUTS |
| *Resources delivered to or consumed by the initiative* | | *The direct products of initiative activities* |
| • staff time | • Discuss and explore vocabulary words from text and robotics concepts | • # of sessions |
| • library books | | • # of books checked out by participants |
| • meeting room | | • list of words explored |
| • high-speed internet connection | • Teams collaboratively build and program robots to complete book-based challenges | • types of robots created |
| • laptops and software | | • creative solutions reached |
| • robot kits | | • photos and videos of students in action |
| • game materials | • Communication and collaboration exercises | |
| • staff development | | • # of volunteer hours |
| • group workspace | | • # of attendees |
| • volunteer time | | • # of new friendships |

**Table 6.2:** Follow the White RabBOT Camp Standards

<table>
<tr><td colspan="3">IMPACT STATEMENT</td></tr>
<tr><td colspan="3">Students rich in traditional and digital literacy</td></tr>
<tr><td colspan="3">OUTCOMES</td></tr>
<tr><td colspan="3">*Benefits for participants during and after activities*</td></tr>
<tr>
<td>Most participants will gain technological knowledge, skills, and abilities.</td>
<td>Most participants will augment technical and linguistic vocabulary.</td>
<td>Most participants will become more comfortable and adept at communicating and collaborating with peers.</td>
</tr>
<tr><td colspan="3">STANDARDS</td></tr>
<tr>
<td></td>
<td>CCSS.ELA-LITERACY.CCRA.L.4 Determine or clarify the meaning of unknown and multiple-meaning words and phrases by using context clues, analyzing meaningful word parts, and consulting general and specialized reference materials, as appropriate.</td>
<td>CCSS.ELA-LITERACY.CCRA.SL.1 Prepare for and participate effectively in a range of conversations and collaborations with diverse partners, building on others' ideas and expressing their own clearly and persuasively.</td>
</tr>
<tr>
<td>AASL 1.1.2 Use prior and background knowledge as context for new learning.</td>
<td>AASL 1.1.4 Find, evaluate, and select appropriate sources to answer questions.</td>
<td>AASL 1.1.9 Collaborate with others to broaden and deepen understanding.</td>
</tr>
<tr>
<td>AASL 1.1.8 Demonstrate mastery of technology tools for accessing information and pursuing inquiry.</td>
<td>AASL 1.1.6 Read, view, and listen for information presented in any format in order to make inferences and gather meaning.</td>
<td>AASL 2.1.5 Collaborate with others to exchange ideas, develop new understandings, make decisions, and solve problems.</td>
</tr>
<tr>
<td></td>
<td></td>
<td>AASL 3.1.2 Participate and collaborate as members of a social and intellectual network of learners.</td>
</tr>
<tr>
<td></td>
<td></td>
<td>AASL 3.2.3 Demonstrate teamwork by working productively with others.</td>
</tr>
<tr>
<td>ISTE 6A Understand and use technology systems.</td>
<td></td>
<td>ISTE 2D Contribute to project teams to produce original works or solve problems.</td>
</tr>
<tr>
<td>ISTE 6D Transfer current knowledge to learning of new technologies.</td>
<td></td>
<td>ISTE 5B Exhibit a positive attitude toward using technology that supports collaboration, learning, and productivity.</td>
</tr>
<tr><td colspan="3">INDICATORS</td></tr>
<tr>
<td>Pre- and post-survey of specific skills</td>
<td>Pre- and post-survey of particular vocabulary words</td>
<td>Observation and pre- and post-survey</td>
</tr>
</table>

# Publicity Description

Below is an example publicity description that may be adapted to suit a library's particular needs:

### *Follow the White RabBOT Camp*

Dig into building and programming robots to accomplish missions based on Lewis Carroll's classic *Alice's Adventures in Wonderland* in this multiday camp. Your team will be counting on you, so make sure you can attend all 4 sessions!

# Time Allotment

Instructors should budget a *minimum* of eight total hours to allow participants to complete most if not all challenges; however, instructors who take advantage all of the literacy extension opportunities provided or those who create their own will likely need to extend the time frame. It is common for the time to be divided into two hours a day for four days. For instance, over the summer, a camp might run 1–3 P.M. Monday–Thursday, or an afterschool series might be two hours a week for four weeks. The amount of time allotted and its division should consider the needs of the age-level served. For instance, two hours a day stretches the attention spans of young children as far as developmentally appropriate, while giving them the time to dig in creatively and become immersed. New Adults, those aged 18–24, may be best served by a day-long workshop.

# Age-Levels

This camp may be adapted for any combination in the 8–24-year-old range. While instructors may group multiple ages together based on local factors, that is, advertising the camp for 8–10-year-olds or 12–14-year-olds, it is important to remember the full dynamics of the experience. For example, while a particular 8-year-old may have advanced technical skills, he may not be developmentally ready to interact well with 12-year-olds.

# Class Size

Robotics events tend to attract a large number and variety of students. It can be tempting to try to extend the opportunity by increasing the registration limit. It is important to remember, however, that smaller class sizes and lower instructor to student ratios allow for more individual attention, which in turn allows for more creativity and deeper exploration. These lessons are also designed for physical involvement of all members of a team. Keeping team sizes small (two to three students) allows for each participant to contribute via a certain job in each challenge, whether as programmer, researcher, or builder.

Of course, those using these activities in a school classroom setting may have limited control over class sizes. One method to keep all students engaged is to utilize a volunteer coach and divide the class into two groups that alternate through the activities. The volunteer might lead Group A through the reading, literacy activities, while the instructor volunteer explains the challenge brief to Group B and assists them with their building, programming, and testing.

# Volunteers

Even with small classes, it can still be a challenge for one adult to effectively support and manage even 12 students in this hands-on, dynamic environment that often includes young people, technology, and numerous small parts. The use of teen or adult volunteers provides some relief to both students and instructors. There are numerous ways to involve volunteers in the leadership of robotics classes, such as documenting the camp through pictures, video, newspaper articles, and blog posts. Volunteers who enjoy performing are a great resource for creative sharing of the text, whether as readers' theatre, puppet show, or play, and those with technical expertise can provide coaching and real-world examples.

## Recruiting Volunteers

To recruit teens, remember that many middle schools and high schools have robotics teams, clubs, or classes, and even those that don't are likely to have technology clubs or other groups that might be used as a launching pad for recruiting. Reach out to advisors of Key Club, National Honor Society, or other groups that require students to complete community service.

Adults may be recruited from engineering firms, companies employing scientists, and local colleges. Though robotics can be intimidating to those without experience, don't be afraid to invite those parents and seniors who are richer in people skills than technology skills. Much of making an experience work is about helping participants to work together, share, collaborate, and think creatively.

## Meaningful Work

Volunteers tend to enjoy helping others when the work is meaningful, and when they are encouraged to contribute their own best talents and ideas. Prior to the robotics class, host an orientation and collaboration session with the volunteers to describe how the camp will work and provide exploratory learning with the robots. Explain how you feel you need assistance and ask for feedback from them as to how they might best contribute. For instance, a volunteer who enjoys organization and order might be the timekeeper and kit manager. Others might contribute best by coaching on building techniques or coding, and still others may serve as cheerleaders and social supports.

## Robots

In Chapter 3, we looked at six types of robot education products available. Each of the products examined possesses the capabilities necessary to complete at least five of the provided challenges. All challenges may be completed using the intermediate level robots, LEGO® MINDSTORMS® or any VEX® robots. Other robot products or robots built from scratch may also be used. The capabilities that a robot needs to possess are listed under the heading of each challenge.

LEGO® MINDSTORMS® and VEX® robots will need to be constructed prior to the first challenge. Both brands provide base model instructions. The base model is easily adaptable by students for various challenges, although some students may elect to rebuild their robot into a custom configuration. Rather than beginning camp with robot construction, which can be tedious and overwhelming to those without context and experience, consider starting camp with Challenge 6, which requires minimal programming and no building for robots with a programmable display.

## Props

In addition to the printable game board, some challenges require props. The prop(s) needed for a particular challenge are indicated under that challenge's heading. All props are inexpensive and readily available items. When possible, it is advisable to provide each team with its own set of props so they may test their solutions freely. Props needed for this camp are:

- Small jars—a jam jar, baby food jar, etc.
- Small nonfragile figurines—ideally a rabbit or lizard but may be a classic plastic army figurine or other similar toy
- Cups—teacups fit the story but disposable cups will work
- Teabags
- Small balls—such as a table tennis ball
- Playing cards

Option A in Challenge 5 requires a tape measure or yardstick. One measuring device per team is preferable if possible.

# Scoring

Each challenge is assigned a base level of points. Instructors may offer additional points for collaboration and creativity. Points are used to create the friendly, motivational environment of a game, rather than to invoke a highly aggressive competition. It is common and desirable for students to disregard points altogether and focus primarily on the satisfaction of accomplishment. If points help some students, stay focused and engaged, great; if not, instructors should feel free to ignore them.

To scale the challenges to learners of all levels, instructors may demand more advanced solutions from students with accelerated knowledge. For instance, a challenge might call for the robot to wave a flag when a whistle blows. Students with minimal experience might program the robot to play a whistle sound, then turn on the motor that will move the flag, whereas more advanced students might program a sound sensor to trigger the motor to turn when it hears a person whistle. Both of these solutions are correct in that they solve the challenge as stated. Both students would earn an equal number of points. Like the handicap system used in golf, this is an attempt to level the playing field.

Advanced students may also be engaged as mentors to teams with less experience. This can help build communication and collaboration skills. The mentees can earn extra points by seeking assistance from their mentor before coming to the instructor, and the mentor can earn points for assisting the mentees.

Lastly, advanced students who have completed the assigned challenge(s) may be engaged by creating a challenge for future camps. This is particularly effective if students document their successful models and programs with photos and written description, augmenting the English Language Arts component of their learning.

# Guide Components

The guide includes similar elements for each challenge including a reading from the text, a description of the challenge, programming considerations, and an example solution.

# Traditional Literacy

The challenges in this camp are based on events in Lewis Carroll's classic *Alice's Adventures in Wonderland*. The rights to this text have passed into the public domain. There are, however, numerous versions of *Alice's Adventures in Wonderland* published in print form that retain some manor of copyright, whether for the illustrations, typesetting, or abridgement/ rendition. Free to use copies of the original text are available to print, read in browser or on a device, from numerous online sources such as Project Gutenberg. Those working with students on the younger end may wish to use an adapted version of the text, as the original text is listed at a 5.9 grade-level rating by Scholastic and a 980 Lexile level by MetaMetrics (Scholastic, 2015).

## Read Together

Before the announcement of each challenge, the class will discover its root in the text by reading the appropriate section. Instructors may read aloud themselves, play from an audiobook recording, or ask for student volunteers. Evade hurt feelings and embarrassment by eschewing "round reading" or mandatory reading aloud. If possible, provide enough copies for teams to follow along in the text, so students can see unfamiliar words in action. This reading time serves not only as research for the challenges, but also as a commercial for the featured book and the joy of reading. It is common for students to want to read the book in its entirety either in class or at home. Instructors are encouraged to provide copies for checkout.

## Vocabulary

Vocabulary words that are introduced in each challenge are defined from *Merriam-Webster's Collegiate Dictionary,* 11th Edition. To build comprehension, however, instructors are encouraged to discuss and define the words as a class from contextual learning and post the terms with their natural language definitions in the classroom for referral and to encourage habitual use. The vocabulary words are selected either from the book or from relevant technology concepts. Instructors may certainly replace or augment the example vocabulary words provided with ones more suited to a particular age group, robot product, or activity.

## *Challenge Brief*

The challenge brief provides language to announce the challenge and any pertinent rules, restrictions, or clarifications; however, all challenges are intentionally left open to interpretation to maximize creative thinking and the opportunity for multiple correct solutions. Instructors are also encouraged to adapt the challenges to the needs of the students or class situation.

## Coding Clues

These guides are flexible enough to accommodate many different types of robots, each using different programming environments, so Coding Clues provide presenters with a logical framework for thinking about programming and examples of how the challenge may be adapted for different types of robot products. Note that there are typically many other potential solutions, and robot products beyond those that are discussed can certainly work.

## One Possible Solution

An example programming solution to each challenge is included to provide some insight to instructors as they coach students. Videos of the solutions in action and building guides for the custom models used in the videos are available from the website listed in the Appendix. Instructors may be tempted to construct a similar model for class demonstration; however, this can lead to copying of the model rather than creative and critical thinking and problem solving. All solutions provided use LEGO® MINDSTORMS® EV3 kits and software except for Option B in Challenge 5, which uses the LEGO® WeDo® base kit and software.

## Challenge 1: Follow the White Rabbit

Beginning the camp, participants without much experience may need some grounding in both the structure of the class and the use of the robots. This first challenge provides an opportunity for both. The challenge is potentially suitable for all mobile robots, and requires only the game board as a prop.

With the exception of LEGO® WeDo®, all robots featured in Chapter 3 of this work are capable of movement across a distance and, so, can complete this challenge. To use a LEGO® WeDo® robot for this challenge, a wheeled chassis will most likely need to be created. The LEGO® WeDo® Extension Kit provides components to do this and instructions for a car build are available from LEGO® Education's website. Because the LEGO® WeDo® must be tethered to the computer to operate, a laptop must move with the robot as it completes the challenge.

## Introduction

After welcoming the participants, explain how the camp will operate. Participants work in pairs or small teams. Each team is assigned a robot and computer (if necessary) with which to program. At each session of camp, one or more challenges are introduced. In the early challenges, instructors provide more guidance as to how to program the robot, but as the camp progresses, teams are encouraged to work together to find their own solutions. The bulk of the camp time, teams work independently with periodic check-ins from the facilitator(s). Teams are encouraged to use the wealth of resources available to them through the library to research possible solutions.

Teams receive points for each challenge completed. Instructors may choose whether to award points on a rolling basis, or whether to hold a competition on the final day of camp during which teams demonstrate their prowess. For younger students it is recommended that points be awarded as achieved or on a daily basis. Older participants may enjoy waiting for a culminating main event with family and friends in attendance.

After explaining that each challenge is based on Lewis Carroll's classic book *Alice's Adventures in Wonderland,* gather participants around the game board (Figure 6.1) to read the first passage and describe the first challenge. This is a very basic challenge, designed to give instructors the opportunity to start at the very beginning with participants.

**Figure 6.1:** Thumbnail of the Follow the White RabBOT Camp Game Board.

# Read Together

Read the first three paragraphs of chapter 1 until the White Rabbit pops "down a large rabbit hole under the hedge."

# Challenge Brief

Program the robot to move from Alice to the rabbit hole, and then stop: 2 points.

Advanced students may be challenged to follow the curves of the landscape.

# Coding Clues

Students may achieve this challenge by simply angling the robot on the board and programming the robot to drive in a straight path, limiting the length that the motor is on by the number of rotations or amount of time.

Students with more experience may program the robot to curve with the landscape by adjusting the power given to a particular wheel (LEGO® MINDSTORMS® and VEX®), drawing the shape of the landscape (Sphero), or using a light or color sensor to determine where to drive and when to stop.

# Robot Basics

Before teaching participants how to use a particular robot, it may be wise to review some basic robot concepts.

◉AASL 1.1.6

*Watch* View a short video such as "What is a Robot" by Hello World or "What is a Robot?" by MonkeySee on YouTube to introduce the concept of robots.

*Discuss* As a group, talk about the three defining characteristics of a robot as discussed in the videos and in chapter 1: brain, senses, and response, or think, sense, act.

*Play Robot or Not Game* All materials available for download.

✚CCSS.ELA-LITERACY.CCRA.SL.2 ❖ ISTE 6A&D ◉AASL 1.1.2, 1.1.9, 2.1.5, 2.2.3, 3.1.2, & 3.2.3 Based on what they've gathered from the videos and group discussion, team members will work together to identify whether the assigned item is a robot or not.

+LITERACY.CCRA.SL.4 ✪AASL 3.1.1 & 3.2.1 Ask teams to share their rationale with the larger group.

## Programming 101

❖ISTE 6A Lead participants through how to program the robot in general and how to specifically program it to move and stop.

+CCSS.ELA-LITERACY.CCRA.L.4 When speaking with students regarding the robots, use actual names of components such as *motor*, *beam*, and *gear,* to create a class culture that uses technical vocabulary in its proper context.

## *One Possible Solution*

Like most of the possible solutions provided throughout this chapter, the following example uses LEGO® MINDSTORMS® EV3 robots and software. This programming solution was created using the basic driving base model.

In this example shown in Figure 6.2, the Move Tank Block powers the robot to move forward for three rotations, or full turns, of the motors connected to the B and C ports, effectively, the wheels. The right (B) wheel moves forward at 50 percent power and the left (C) wheel moves forward at 45 percent power. This discrepancy causes the robot to angle to the left, toward the lower powered wheel because the right wheel is covering more ground at a fast rate. This angle aligns with the angle of the landscape on the board. In the next Move Tank Block, the discrepancy is reversed so that the robot angles back toward the right, as the landscape on the board moves slightly back uphill. Notice that the discrepancy is larger in the second block. This is because when the second block begins, the robot is already at a downward angle to the edge of the board, and the

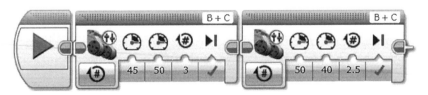

**Figure 6.2:** Follow the White Rabbit Possible Program

power difference must increase to return the robot back to parallel with the board, and then slightly past into an upward angle.

This is a perfect example of the type of multifaceted learning for which robotics are so perfectly suited. Those not confident in math concepts themselves might partner with a colleague to take advantage of the potential expansion into geometry and other math fields that are in play throughout the challenges.

## Language Learning

✦ CCSS.ELA-LITERACY.CCRA.SL.1 ✪AASL 1.1.6 Challenge participants to define the terms below in their own words.

Each group may be assigned one term, or each group may receive all four and then the large group can discuss and compile.

✦CCSS.ELA-LITERACY.CCRA.L4 & L6 Encourage teams to research terms using dictionaries, thesauri, or other library resources.

*Hardware—the physical parts of a computer system*
*Software—the programs, including the operating system, used by a computer*
*Program—(noun) instructions written in any one of many coding languages that enable operation of a computer*
*Autonomous—functioning independently of external control*

# Challenge 2: Down the Rabbit Hole

This challenge expands on the programming knowledge gained in the first challenge and introduces custom design. This challenge requires a prop, such as a small jam jar or baby food jar.

## Read Together

Read the next four paragraphs of chapter 1, from "In another moment down went Alice after it," through to "Why, I wouldn't say anything about it, even if I fell off the top of the house!"

## Language Learning

✦ CCSS.ELA-LITERACY.CCRA.SL.1 ✪AASL 1.1.6, 1.1.8, 2.1.5, 3.1.2, & 3.2.3 ❖ISTE 2A, 5B, & 6A

Marmalade Master—The Great Debate

Since the 2014 release of the Paddington Bear movie, marmalade has been making a comeback. People are buying more and making their own. Each team will research marmalade recipes to identify what element or elements are *essential* for marmalade, then find or create a marmalade recipe that the team members think is the best, and prepare their persuasive arguments. At the end of the preparation time, each team will have 30 seconds to present. Visual aides are welcome.

There is a twist, however. Team members must communicate with each other silently during prep time. They may use written messages, hand gestures, or other nonverbal methods.

Students may vote for the best argument (other than their own team's), or facilitator and volunteers may vote. Points may be awarded for the number of votes received, or the lucidity of the arguments, and may also take into consideration how well team members collaborated.

As a group, discuss how participants found the experience. What are some of the benefits of communicating nonverbally? What are some of the difficulties? This exercise is designed to help team members develop awareness of each other's communication preferences and styles and help strengthen team dynamics.

*Marmalade*—(noun) *a type of fruit preserve in which the fruit and its rind are suspended in jelly*

*Essential*—(adjective) *something vital to achievement of an object's function, cause, or purpose*

## Challenge Brief

Program the robot to move the marmalade jar from its original spot at the top of the well to the cupboard: 2 points.

Advanced participants may be challenged to continue to the bottom of the well without disturbing the jar after it is placed in the cupboard.

## Coding Clues

Students may achieve this challenge by programming the robot to drive on a slightly curved path, pushing the jam jar with the robot, and limiting the length that the motor is on by the number of rotations or amount of time. Depending on the type of robot used, students may need to build on to the robot. For instance, Sphero might need to be placed in a chariot, so that an arm may be built from bricks to direct the jar.

This challenge may likely be best completed with only slight adjustments to a basic drive forward program, similar to that which was used in the first challenge; however, some students may want to use sensors. Because the well section of the board is quite dark, and the contrast minimal between the landing stations, it is unlikely that a typical color or light sensor will be able to detect the difference. A gyro sensor might be useful to determine the angle necessary and program the robot accordingly; however, this may be an overly complicated solution to a simple problem. Encourage students to find the simplest solution possible, using only those programming and custom build elements that are *essential*.

❖ ISTE 2D, 6A, & 6D

Invite teams to look at each element of their previous program and see what might be adjusted to adapt the program for a different angle and distance.

## One Possible Solution

In the example shown in Figure 6.3, the first Move Tank Block is set to On for Degrees. It is important to note that degrees, in this case, refers to the number of degrees in a rotation, rather than the angle taken by the robot, so 360 degrees would equate one full rotation of the wheel. In this example, the block is set for 800 degrees, approximately 2.2 rotations of the wheel. Students can determine the distance from the jam jar to the cupboard through trial and error, by rolling the robot over the course and observing the rotations of the white pointer on the wheel, or by using the Port View app on the brick interface to track the degrees travelled.

The second Move Tank Block creates a backward pivot turn by removing power from the right wheel, and setting the left wheel power to negative 30. In the EV3 programming software, negative numbers are used to reverse direction of the rotation. In the third Move Tank Block, the robot moves straight forward to navigate past the jam jar. The fourth block

**Figure 6.3:** Down the Rabbit Hole Possible Program

once again uses the differential to turn the robot slightly toward the lower powered wheel, in this case, to the right, to angle the robot back toward the center of the bottom of the well.

This programming solution is designed for the basic EV3 driving base with the addition of the extension found on page 54 of the EV3 building guide. This approximately three-inch extension is used as a plow to move the marmalade jar, with a Left Curved Panel piece added as a guard on the left side. Those using differently sized plows may need to adjust the number of rotations in the program.

# Challenge 3: Curiouser and Curiouser . . .

This challenge requires a robot that can be programmed to expand and contract some of its parts. All LEGO® and VEX® robots possess the necessary components. No props are required for this challenge.

## Read Together

Read the end of chapter 1 from, "Alice was not a bit hurt" through the first two paragraphs of chapter 2 that end with, "Oh dear, what nonsense I'm talking."

## Language Learning

✦ CCSS.ELA-LITERACY.CCRA.L.4 ❖ AASL 1.1.6 & 1.1.9 A Curious Large Group Discussion

This activity is intended to help students better understand the multiple ways in which the word *curious* may be used.

*Curious*—A: *disposed to inquire and discover*

Reread the following quote: "Alice started to her feet, for it flashed across her mind that she had never before seen a rabbit with either a waist-coat-pocket, or a watch to take out of it, and, burning with *curiosity*, she ran across the field after it, and was just in time to see it pop down a large rabbit-hole under the hedge."

Ask the students, "Why do you think Alice was curious about the White Rabbit?" and "What does it mean to feel curious?"

*Curious*—B: *unusual, atypical, or unexpected*

Later, after Alice takes the DRINK ME bottle she says, "What a curious feeling! . . . I must be shutting up like a telescope." Ask students, "How do you think it would feel to suddenly start shrinking?"

*Curious A or B?*

Ask students, "Which meaning of *curious* do you think she means at the beginning of chapter 2?" "Curiouser and cursiouser!" cried Alice (she was so much surprised, that for the moment she quite forgot how to speak good English)"

# Challenge Brief

Have the robot move to the table with the DRINK ME bottle: shrink and then grow: 4 points.

Facilitators may determine, based on skill and age level of participants, and the type of robots used, whether the entire robot needs to shrink and grow or if a part, such as an attached arm is sufficient.

# Coding Clues

❖ ISTE 6A & 6D This is an engineering challenge that requires programming and customized building to complement each other. Typically, at least one motor is used to drive the chassis and another motor is used to power the expandable and collapsible elements.

Because LEGO® WeDo® sets only include one motor, the challenge will likely need to be adapted for those using this model so that the robot does not need to drive to the table.

❖ ISTE 1A & B There are no parameters on how the robot needs to grow and shrink (for instance, it could grow horizontally rather than vertically), so encourage students to be creative and take their existing knowledge further.

❖ ISTE 2D, 4D, & 5B ✪AASL 4.4.2 & 4.4.3 Discuss with students how it takes people of all interests and skills to create robots in the real world. Electrical and mechanical engineers, computer programmers, visual designers, and more each contribute their talents. Invite teams to identify how they will work together on this challenge. What roles will they fill? Will one participant be the lead builder and another the lead programmer? These roles can change with each challenge.

# One Possible Solution

This program, shown in two parts in Figures 6.4 and 6.5, is longer because it includes some fun additions like sound effects and text. These elements are not necessary to complete the challenge as stated but demonstrate the ways in which students may express themselves creatively.

The first block simply moves the robot from the bottom of the well to the table. Next, on the Display Block, the Text Grid mode indicates the robot will display text, and that the location of the text will be based on a grid. Once a text mode is selected, custom text may be entered in the upper right corner of the block. The Clear Screen parameter is marked as true so that any existing text on the screen would be erased prior to displaying this new text, rather than this new text adding to what is already present. The X and Y parameters indicate where the text is to be plotted on the screen's grid. The Wait Block following the Display Block is in Time mode and keeps the text on the screen for one second.

After the Wait Block, the program splits into two strands, so that two things happen simultaneously. One is that the Sound Block plays the Magic Wand sound effect, one of the sounds that automatically install as part of the EV3 software, and the robot begins to shrink. The second is

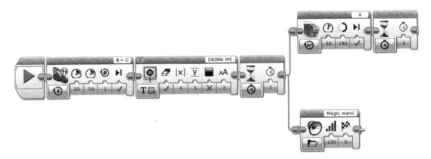

**Figure 6.4:** Curiouser and Curiouser Possible Program Part 1

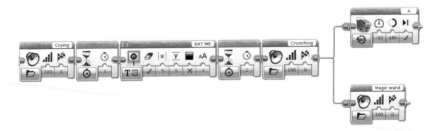

**Figure 6.5:** Curiouser and Curiouser Possible Program Part 2

that the robot begins to shrink by lowering the extension attached to the medium motor in port A.

After a one-second wait, the next Sound Block is set to the Crying sound effect to mimic Alice's reaction when she realizes that she forgot the key on the top of the table. At this point in the story, the cakes appear, and likewise in the program, after a one-second wait, the Display Block issues the words on the cakes, *EAT ME*. The two-second Wait Block after this allows viewers time to read the words before they disappear. The Crunching sound effect produced from the Sound Block represents Alice eating the cakes. The program then, once again splits so that the Magic Wand sound effect can be played simultaneously with the robot growing again via the motorized attachment connected to Port A.

# Challenge 4: In a Little Bill

There are two options for this challenge. Any LEGO® or VEX® robots should be adaptable for either option. Option A requires a robot that can launch an item upward. Ideally, this would be a small, nonbreakable, lizard figurine, but another small object, such as the ball that will be used in Challenge 9 will work. Note that the selected item will be moving through the air with some force, so avoid sharp edges.

Option B requires a robot that can capture an item, such as claw. This option also requires a prop. Ideally, this would be a white rabbit figurine, but it could be any stand in toy or small nonfragile item.

## Read Together

Read from the beginning of chapter 4 through, "They all made a rush at Alice the moment she appeared; but she ran off as hard as she could, and soon found herself safe in a thick wood."

## Challenge Brief

Option A: Kick "Bill" out the chimney. Launch the item representing Bill into the air: 3 points. Extra points may be awarded based on achieved height, velocity, or angle.

Option B: Make a grab for the rabbit: 2 points for making a mechanism that can make a clasping motion, 5 points for capturing the rabbit, 7 points for locating the rabbit using one or more sensors.

# Coding Clues

Both of these options rely more on clever engineering than on programming.

❂AASL 1.1.8 ❖ISTE 2D, 6A, & 6D Those with creativity and tenacity may be able to find and adapt ideas from the online community or create their own models that shoot the Bill prop straight into the air like a rocket.

❂AASL 1.1.8 ❖ISTE 2D, 6A, & 6D Option B is particularly suited to the VEX® Clawbot, or using the arm build from the LEGO® MINDSTORMS® EV3 GRIPP3R model. It is, however, quite possible to create a motion-sensing claw using a LEGO® WeDo® set.

# One Possible Solution

A simple solution for Option A is to create an arm, or in this case, foot, that rotates using the Medium Motor. The program shown in Figure 6.6 is only one block long, and the power is set to 100, the maximum, to try to create enough momentum to launch the Bill figurine into the air. The foot design is curved with a lip to potentially catch on the figurine and scoop it upward.

The example for Option B (Figure 6.7) becomes more complex because the Ultrasonic Sensor is used to determine when to close the claw hand. The first block within the loop is a Switch Block that is set to the Ultrasonic Sensor Compare mode. The parameters on this block have the Ultrasonic Sensor take a reading to determine if the statement "The sensor detects an object within two inches" is true or false. If the sensor detects an object within the set distance, then the argument becomes *true* and the top portion happens. The robot stops moving because rotations are turned off on the large motors via ports B and C, and the medium motor in port A turns on for 180 degrees, which closes the claw. The

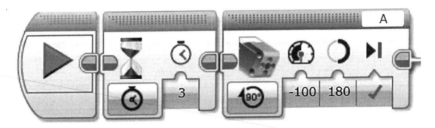

**Figure 6.6:** In a Little Bill Option A Possible Program

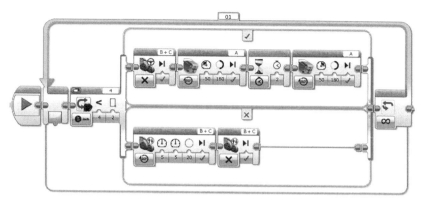

**Figure 6.7:** In a Little Bill Option B Possible Program

claw remains shut for two seconds due to the Wait Block, and then opens, releasing the rabbit figurine. If the sensor does not detect an object within two inches, then the argument is *false*, and then the bottom portion happens. The Move Tank Block moves the robot slowly forward at 5 percent power for a brief 20 degrees and then stops. The loop sends the program back to the beginning, so the Ultrasonic Sensor looks for an object again, and the switch cycle repeats.

It is important to note that the Ultrasonic Sensor cannot determine the difference between types of objects. Like a bat, it simply sends out a sound wave and then "listens" for the ping back to determine the distance of any nearby objects. Humans can't hear the sounds waves because of the frequency of the pitch. Challenges using an Ultrasonic Sensor provide opportunities to discuss the physics involved and to bring in a community expert.

# *Language Learning*

+CCSS.ELA-LITERACY.CCRA.SL.1 ✪AASL 1.1.9, 2.1.5 Challenge participants to define the terms below in their own words.

Each group may be assigned one term, or each group may receive all four and then the large group can discuss and compile.

+CCSS.ELA-LITERACY.CCRA.L4 & L6 ✪AASL 1.1.4 & 1.1.5

Encourage teams to research terms using dictionaries, thesauri, or other library resources.

*Launch*—(verb) *to release or put in motion*

*Projectile*—(noun) *an object put into motion by external force*

# Challenge 5: Who Are You?

All of the robot products discussed in Chapter 3 will support at least one of the options provided in this challenge with the exception of Bee-Bot. This challenge does not require props; however, for Option A, a measuring tool such as a tape measure or yardstick is necessary to confirm success.

## Read Together

Read chapter 5 through to the end of the Caterpillar section, at which point Alice eats a bit of each side of the mushroom.

## Language Learning

+CCSS.ELA-LITERACY.CCRA.SL.1 ✪AASL 1.1.9, 2.1.5 Challenge participants to define the terms below in their own words. Each group may be assigned one term, or each group may receive all four and then the large group can discuss and compile.

+CCSS.ELA-LITERACY.CCRA.L4 & L6 ✪AASL 1.1.4 & 1.1.5

Encourage teams to research terms using dictionaries, thesauri, or other library resources.

*Chrysalis—the pupa state in the transition from caterpillar to butterfly, or the case surrounding the pupa*

*Transition—(noun) the process of changing from one state to another (verb) to change states*

## Challenge Brief

Option A: Alice may have avoided offending the Caterpillar if she had known that his height was the same as her own. Create a robot that can measure the length of a person when he or she is lying down. Use a tape measure or yardstick to confirm the accuracy of the reading.

Option B: Alice knows that the Caterpillar will *transition* through a big physical change one day. Create wings that flap like a butterfly.

## Coding Clues

✪AASL 1.1.2 ❖ISTE 1A, 1B, 2D, 6A, & 6D Option A does not specify how the measurement needs to be reported, so a simple solution for those using VEX® and LEGO® MINDSTORMS® is to have the robot report the length in wheel rotations. If facilitators want to provide a bigger challenge, they may require the report to use inches or millimeters, which is perfectly achievable on either platform. Of course, the tricky thing is for the robot to know when to start and stop the measurement. There are several sensor options, but perhaps the most obvious is an Ultrasonic Sensor. The sensor may be placed perpendicular to the chassis and the programming may trigger the measurement to begin and last while the Ultrasonic Sensor detects that it is within a specified distance of another object, in this case, the subject. Sphero will have to be started and stopped by an operator at the ends of the subject, but it may measure and report distance using original programming or the Measuring Tape app available from Google Play.

✪AASL 1.1.2 ❖ ISTE 1A, 1B, 2D, 6A, & 6D Option B probably won't work with Sphero, but it should with most of the other robot products. Note that Cubelets will most likely require the brick adapter and a plethora of brick pieces to accomplish this challenge.

## One Possible Solution

The example program for Option A, split into two parts in Figures 6.8 and 6.9, begins with a three-second Wait Block to make sure all parties are situated. Once the Ultrasonic Sensor detects an object within 30 inches, the loop begins. In the loop, the Move Tank Block moves the robot forward slowly at 10 percent power. The loop stops when the Ultrasonic Sensor no longer detects an object within 30 inches.

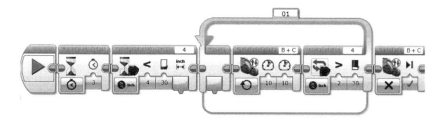

**Figure 6.8:** Who Are You Option A Possible Program Part 1

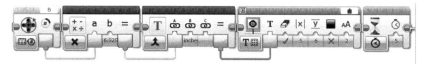

**Figure 6.9:** Who Are You Option A Possible Program Part 2

**Figure 6.10:** Who Are You Option B Possible Program

The B and C ports are then turned off to stop the robot from rotating any further. The Motor Rotation Sensor Block then counts the number of rotations travelled during the program so far. The motor rotation sensor is built into the Large Motors to provide this type of data.

A wire then connects from the number of rotations parameter to the *a* variable parameter in the adjacent Math Block. The number in the *b* variable parameter is 6.929137611 which represents the circumference of the wheel in inches (17.6 cm). Multiplying the number of rotations by the circumference of the wheel provides the full distance in inches travelled by the robot. This value is than merged into a Text Block, so that the descriptor of *inches* may be added. The full phrase is than wired to the Display Block that will show the length travelled, or the length of the person, in inches. The Wait Block allows this information to remain on the screen for five seconds.

This challenge presents a great opportunity to incorporate math learning. Instead of providing students with the circumference, instructors might challenge students to measure the diameter of the wheel and then find the circumference by multiplying that number by pi.

The example shown in Figure 6.10 for Option B utilizes the LEGO® WeDo® base kit and software. In this loop, the first block sets the motor at a power level of 3, roughly 30 percent power. The next block tells the motor to turn clockwise, and the third block sets the duration of the motor. These steps are then repeated, but with the alteration of the direction of the motor to counterclockwise. On the build, the wings are connected to gears that turn in opposite directions of one another when the motor is on. This challenge presents the opportunity to talk with students about gears and how the intermeshed teeth of the connected gears will turn them in alternating directions.

# Challenge 6: Cheshire Cat

This challenge is easily adaptable for all discussed robot platforms. It may be a good challenge with which to start a new or inexperienced group. No props are required, although markers and paper may be necessary for some solutions.

## Read Together

Midway through chapter 6, start reading from, "The Cat only grinned when it saw Alice." Continue through to the end of the chapter.

## Language Learning

✚CCSS.ELA-LITERACY.CCRA.L.4

*Mad*

Some definitions from *Merriam-Webster's Collegiate Dictionary* for the word *mad* are:

1. *carried away by intense anger: FURIOUS*

2. *disordered in mind: INSANE*

3. *carried away by enthusiasm or desire*

Discuss as a large group: Which definition do you think the Cheshire Cat means when he describes himself as mad?

✚CCSS.ELA-LITERACY.CCRA.L.4 ✪AASL 1.1.4, 1.1.6, 1.1.8, 1.1.9, & 2.1.5 ❖ISTE 2D, 5B

In teams, participants use library resources to complete the *Mad, Mad or Mad Match Up* downloadable activity sheet, determining which use of the word *mad* is intended in the examples.

✚CCSS.ELA-LITERACY.CCRA.SL.1 ✪AASL 1.1.2, 1.1.6, 1.1.9, & 3.1.2 ❖ISTE 2D, 6A

In teams, choose one definition of mad to represent through the robot. Other teams will try to guess whether your robot is mad, mad or mad.

## Challenge Brief

Look both ways, and then grin: 2 points.

## Coding Clues

Those using robots without programmable displays may need to take a more physical approach. The robot could turn to one direction, then

**Figure 6.11:** Cheshire Cat Possible Program

the other, and then drive in the shape of a grin or draw a grin with an attached marker.

## One Possible Solution

In the example shown in Figure 6.11, the three-second Wait Block is optional to build suspense before the "Cheshire cat" appears. The Display Blocks use images from the expressions folder. Note that Image Mode must be selected on the Display Blocks for the image options to appear in the drop-down menus on the top right corner of the blocks. The Wait Block following each Display Block keeps the image on the screen for the designated number of seconds.

# Challenge 7: Mad Tea Party

This challenge requires the ability to hoist and lower an item. VEX®, LEGO® MINDSTORMS® and WeDo® robot kits all include the necessary parts in order to this. Props needed for this challenge include a teabag and a cup.

## Read Together

Read chapter 7 in its entirety.

## Language Learning

✚CCSS.ELA-LITERACY.CCRA.SL.1 ✪AASL 1.1.2, 1.1.9, 2.1.5, & 3.1.2 ❖ISTE 2D

When Alice claims that "I mean what I say" is the same thing as "I say what I mean," the Mad Hatter and company provide several examples of how reversing the verb order changes the meaning of the sentence. As a large group, discuss why this is for each example, and then challenge each team to collaborate on the funniest or most absurd possible example.

Each team will fill in the following sentence:

Why, you might just as well say that I (verb a) what I (verb b) is the same thing as I (verb b) what I (verb a).

For example: Why, you might just as well say that I spill what I drink is the same thing as I drink what I spill.

## Challenge Brief

Dunk a teabag into the teacup: 3 points.

## Coding Clues

✪AASL 1.1.2 ❖ISTE 1A, 1B, 2D, 6A, & 6D This challenge presents an opportunity to introduce the concept of a pulley. The teabag string may be placed in the pulley groove. With the tag end secured, the teabag will raise and lower with the turning of the pulley. This solution requires minimal programming if the apparatus is placed directly over the cup. More advanced students with mobile robots may be challenged to dunk the teabag when the robot reaches the cup. An additional challenge may be to actually make a cup of tea, by lowering the teabag into hot water, and timing its removal to the brew time of the tea.

*Pulley—*(noun) *a wheel that transfers energy through a belt that rotates around its indented edge*

*Belt—*(noun) *a strip of malleable material that connects to itself around at least one pulley*

## One Possible Solution

In addition to the basic EV3 driving base, this example, divided between Figures 6.12 and 6.13, uses one custom apparatus to place the Medium

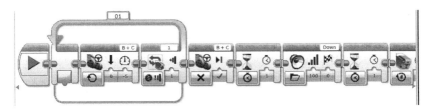

**Figure 6.12:** Mad Tea Party Possible Program Part 1

**Figure 6.13:** Mad Tea Party Possible Program Part 2

Motor, connected pulley, and teacup high above any potential cup. A second custom component, aligned with the teabag, is designed to bump the touch sensor when it collides with a cup. Because both elements are attached at the back of the driving base, the Move Steering Block at the beginning of the program drives the robot slowly backward at 5 percent power. The loop ends when the touch sensor is bumped, that is, when the cup is in range. The next block ensures that the large motors stop immediately after the bump, rather than coasting. The one-second Wait Block allows everything to settle for a moment before continuing.

Though unnecessary to complete the challenge as stated, Sound Blocks are included in the program just for fun. The first Sound Block announces the upcoming motion, and the Wait Block pauses the program for one second. The Medium Motor Block turns the motor connected to port A. The axle inserted in the Medium Motor Block turns the pulley around which the teabag string is wrapped, lowering the attached bag into the cup. Next, a five second Wait Block represents the time to brew the tea, typically three to five minutes in reality, and then a Sound Block announces the ensuing upward motion of the bag. Then, the Ready sound effect is played to announce the completion of the tea.

# Challenge 8: Painting the Roses Red

This challenge is suitable for all LEGO® and VEX® robots and Sphero with adaptation. Only the game board is required. If it is necessary to print the game board in gray scale, the challenge is still achievable with the robots sensing dark or light in lieu of color.

## *Read Together*

Read chapter 8 from the beginning through the procession of the King and Queen of Hearts ending with Alice's reflection that there would be no point for a procession "if people had all to lie down on their faces, so that they couldn't see it."

# Challenge Brief

Find and announce a red rose: 5 points.

# Coding Clues

❂AASL 1.1.2 ❖ISTE 1A, 1B, 2D, 6A, & 6D One solution for participants using a LEGO® MINDSTORMS®, VEX® or others robot with sensors, is to program it to move in a circular motion, spiraling out from the center of the tree, until the color sensor picks up a change in color on the game board. When the color sensor detects red, the robot will pause in motion and announce the color. This announcement may be done visually using text on the display, or audibly.

For Sphero, the announcement of the color of the rose may be changing color to indicate the rose's color. Sphero does not have a color sensor, so the driver controlling the remote would navigate the robot to move to and stop at the rose.

# One Possible Solution

In the example in Figure 6.14, the program inside the loop begins with a Switch Block using the Color Sensor-Compare-Color mode set to a parameter of Red. If true, the program moves to the top level, and a Sound Block announces the word *red*. If false, the program moves to the bottom level with a Sound Block set to Stop mode, so the robot says nothing.

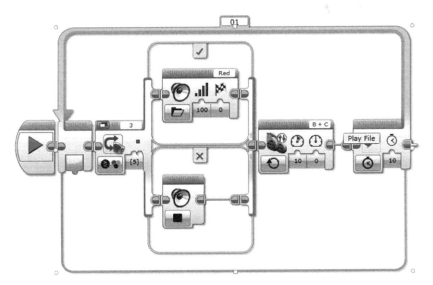

**Figure 6.14:** Painting the Roses Red Possible Program

The Move Tank Block moves in a slow pivot turn around the right wheel, so that the color sensor, directly in front of the right wheel rotates in a small circle, roughly the size and shape of the rose tree on the board. The loop is set to repeat 10 times to give the sensor 10 readings to find the red rose.

# Challenge 9: Flamingo Croquet

There are two options for this challenge so that all robot products discussed in Chapter 3 may achieve this challenge in some manner. Option A requires only the game board, and Option B requires a deck of playing cards and at least one small ball such as a table tennis ball.

## Read Together

In chapter 8, continue reading from the end of the procession until the croquet game when Alice thinks, "They're dreadfully fond of beheading people here: the great wonder is that there's any one left alive."

## Challenge Brief

Option A: Knock a ball through a card wicket. Facilitators may designate the design of the card wicket, or allow teams to create their own. Facilitators may challenge participants to setup a mini croquet course with the cards through which the robots will play. Teams may earn a bonus point for each wicket conquered.

Option B: The robot will represent a hedgehog and drive consecutively over each card wicket printed on the board.

## Coding Clues

✪AASL 1.1.2 ❖ISTE 1A, 1B, 2D, 6A, & 6D Option A is viable for those using robots such as VEX® and LEGO® MINDSTORMS® and WeDo® that may truly replicate a croquet mallet striking a ball through a wicket. The most common solution is to add a rotating arm that will serve as the mallet. Teams looking for an extra challenge may add a sensor to locate the ball that is to be hit.

For Sphero, Cubelets, and Bee-Bot, and robots that do not lend themselves to custom building of a mechanical arm, Option B may be the simplest choice.

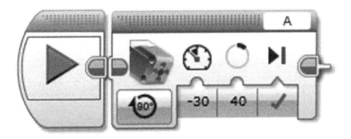

**Figure 6.15:** Flamingo Croquet Possible Program

## *One Possible Solution*

The example shown in Figure 6.15 is a minor adaptation of that used in Option A of the fourth challenge, but the power and duration of the rotation has been adjusted to reflect the lighter weight of the object being struck and the goal to roll it on the ground rather than launch into the air. Students may also wish to adjust the attached arm to reflect these nuances as well.

## Challenge 10: Bank to Bank

Participants often anxiously await this challenge that finally makes use of the enticing black line that flows through the board. This challenge is possible for all mobile robots and requires no additional props.

## *Read Together*

No reading is necessary for this challenge, as it is the culminating challenge representing the whole of the story. Those wishing to begin with reading might use chapter 12, which ends with Alice back on the bank, but keep in mind that choosing to leave the story unfinished at the end of the camp may entice some participants to check out and read the entire book.

## *Challenge Brief*

Alice's adventure begins and ends on the bank of the river. Start your robot from Alice's blanket, travel down the hill, into the rabbit hole and then back up to the bank, following the path: 5 points.

# Coding Clues

⊘AASL 1.1.2 ❖ISTE 2D, 6A, & 6D Robots with a sensor capable of distinguishing between two different values, such as the color sensors available with VEX® and LEGO® MINDSTORMS® may be programmed to follow the line using these sensors.

Robots without such sensors, like the Bee-Bot and Sphero can; however, be programmed to move in a pattern that aligns with the path.

Some students may be able to use distance sensors to get a Cubelet robot to follow a path, but it may require more Cubelets per team than fiscally manageable. Students may certainly direct a Cubelet robot to follow a guiding hand that hovers over the path.

LEGO® WeDo® robots would require a wheeled chassis (built from the extension kit or other LEGO® pieces) to complete this challenge as well as following along the course with the tethered laptop.

# One Possible Solution

Following a line is one of the basic functions of many robots, including the LEGO® MINDSTORMS® EV3 models. In the EV3 software Lobby, select the Robot Educator Menu then Beyond Basics and Switch to view instructions for one program method to follow a black line.

Compared to the stand-alone class, the extended time frame of a camp allows for a deeper dive into robot mechanics, programming, and technical and linguistic vocabulary. Perhaps one of the camp's greatest benefits, however, is the increased opportunity for social exchange. As discussed in Chapter 1, employers increasingly prize communication and collaboration skills, and AASL, ISTE, and the Common Core State Standards all emphasize group productivity, problem solving, and effective idea sharing. In the next chapter, we'll take social learning and collaboration to the next level with a reoccurring club that connects participants with peers, community members and a digital network of experts and resources.

# CHAPTER 7

# Club Activity Guide

The activities in this chapter are designed to be experienced over several sessions, such as multiple class periods, after-school club sessions, or monthly meet-ups. For the sake of brevity, the term *club* is used throughout. Some individual badge challenges may also be used in stand-alone classes, camps, or other settings.

The Appendix provides the link for numerous downloadable, printable resources such badge descriptions, activity sheets, logic models, and outcome measurement tools. The club activities may be achieved with customizable robotics products or self-built robots.

## Preparation and Structure

Though several of the challenges might be used together to form a camp or mini series, if used as a full club, the structure of the event will be quite different from that used in the other guides. It is expected that those leading the club will have started by offering classes or camps, and the participants will have participated in these events. It is understood, however, that particularly in the public library environment, it may be difficult to require prerequisites, so the club builds in some opportunity to introduce basic robotics concepts.

The spirit of camaraderie and continuous learning common to robotics teams inspires the club design, and thus it is intended to create and engage a group of peers who meet regularly. Students will work in small teams that will both contest and support each other. Early badge activities provide some basic skill building, while later badges are designed for more independent exploration, and they incorporate a real-world scenario. To complete the real-world elements, students will likely need to work together independently, beyond club time. To earn a badge, students will need to both complete the technical challenge and document process. The full club experience is intentionally intense in both time commitment and student-driven learning to create a richer, socially supported, connected learning environment, so potential coaches must carefully consider the ongoing responsibility involved.

## Outcomes

The activities in the club are designed to support progress toward the ✚CCSS-ELA Anchor Standards, ❖ISTE Technology Standards, and the ✪AASL Standards for the 21st Century Learner. Some of the standards that are specifically targeted are cited in the logic model (Table 7.1), listed fully in Table 7.2 and highlighted throughout the guide; however, many others are addressed, and facilitators may certainly expand activities to include more. The three outcomes are:

1. Most participants will form supportive relationships that mutually nurture personal interests.

2. Most participants will increase their ability to acquire new knowledge.

3. Most participants will improve their ability to create and share knowledge.

## Publicity Description

Below is an example publicity description that may be adapted to suit a library's particular needs:

*Robot Club: Yellow Brick Quest*

Your mission awaits! Build and program custom robots to conquer challenges from Oz and in your community. Whether you're a tech wizard, creative genius, or average Joe, your team will be counting on you, so make sure you can attend most meetings.

## Time Allotment

Instructors should budget a *minimum* of 24 total hours of club time to allow participants to complete most if not all challenges. Public librarians may wish to schedule the club as monthly, two-hour meetings, and school librarians might put the whole club into one quarter or semester. However, a library decides to divide the scheduled in-club time, it is

**Table 7.1:** Robot Club: Yellow Brick Quest Logic Model

IMPACT STATEMENT

Connected community of learners

OUTCOMES

*Benefits for participants during and after activities*

| | | |
|---|---|---|
| Participants will form supportive relationships that mutually nurture personal interests.<br><br>CCSS.ELA-LITERACY.CCRA.SL.1<br><br>AASL 1.1.9, 3.1.2, 3.2.2, 4.3.1<br><br>ISTE 2A | Most participants will increase their ability to acquire new knowledge.<br><br>CCSS.ELA-LITERACY. CCRA.R.7, R.10, SL.2, W.7<br><br>AASL 1.1.4, 1.1.6, 2.1.1 ISTE 3B, 4A | Most participants will improve their ability to create and share knowledge.<br><br>CCSS.ELA-LITERACY. CCRA.SL.5, W.2, W.6, W.8<br><br>AASL 2.1.6, 3.1.4, 3.3.4, 4.1.7<br><br>ISTE 2C |
| | ACTIVITIES<br><br>*What the initiative does with the inputs to fulfill its mission* | |
| → | | → |
| INPUTS<br><br>*Resources delivered to or consumed by the initiative* | "Yellow Brick Quest" | OUTPUTS<br><br>*The direct products of initiative activities* |
| • Books<br>• Robot components<br>• Computers<br>• Internet connection<br>• Instructor<br>• Props and materials<br>• Community members<br>• Local newspapers or forums<br>• Focus groups or community leaders<br>• Volunteer mentors<br>• Event space<br>• Staff time<br>• Publicity<br>• Web hosting | Build and program robots to complete challenges based on *The Wizard of Oz.*<br><br>Create prototype solutions to assist local clients<br><br>Create prototype solutions to solve community problems<br><br>Lead or assist with community event<br><br>Publish new knowledge | • Original designs<br>• Photos and videos of solutions<br>• Prototypes<br>• Research summaries<br>• # clients<br>• # club participants<br>• # community attendance at feedback sessions<br>• # feedback sessions<br>• # attendees at community event<br>• Blog posts<br>• # of blog responses |

important to remember that individual teams will likely need access to the library as a meeting place and research center in between meetings.

# Age-Levels

This club may be adapted for any combination in the 8–24-year-old range; however, it is probably best suited for tweens, teens, and adults.

**Table 7.2:** Robot Club: Yellow Brick Quest Standards

IMPACT STATEMENT

Connected community of learners

OUTCOMES

| | | |
|---|---|---|
| Most participants will form supportive relationships that mutually nurture personal interests. | Most participants will increase their ability to acquire new knowledge. | Most participants will improve their ability to create and share knowledge. |
| CCSS.ELA-LITERACY.CCRA.SL.1 Prepare for and participate effectively in a range of conversations and collaborations with diverse partners, building on others' ideas and expressing their own clearly and persuasively. | CCSS.ELA-LITERACY.CCRA.R.7 Integrate and evaluate content presented in diverse media and formats, including visually and quantitatively, as well as in words. CCSS.ELA-LITERACY.CCRA.R.10 Read and comprehend complex literary and informational texts independently and proficiently. CCSS.ELA-LITERACY.CCRA.SL.2 Integrate and evaluate information presented in diverse media and formats, including visually, quantitatively, and orally. CCSS.ELA-LITERACY.CCRA.W.7 Conduct short as well as more sustained research projects based on focused questions, demonstrating understanding of the subject under investigation. | CCSS.ELA-LITERACY.CCRA.SL.5 Make strategic use of digital media and visual displays of data to express information and enhance understanding of presentations. CCSS.ELA-LITERACY.CCRA.W.2 Write informative/explanatory texts to examine and convey complex ideas and information clearly and accurately through the effective selection, organization, and analysis of content. CCSS.ELA-LITERACY.CCRA.W.6 Use technology, including the Internet, to produce and publish writing and to interact and collaborate with others. CCSS.ELA-LITERACY.CCRA.W.8 Gather relevant information from multiple print and digital sources, assess the credibility and accuracy of each source, and integrate the information while avoiding plagiarism. |
| AASL 1.1.9 Collaborate with others to broaden and deepen understanding. AASL 3.1.2 Participate and collaborate as members of a social and intellectual network of learners. | AASL 1.1.4 Find, evaluate, and select appropriate sources to answer questions. AASL 1.1.6 Read, view, and listen for information presented in any format in order to make inferences and gather meaning. | AASL 2.1.6 Use the writing process, media and visual literacy, and technology skills to create products that express new understandings. AASL 3.1.4 Use technology and other information tools to organize and display knowledge in ways that others can view, use, and access. AASL 3.3.4 Create products that apply to authentic, real-world contexts. |

| AASL 3.2.2 Show social responsibility by participating actively with others in learning situations and by contributing questions and ideas during group discussions. | AASL 2.1.1 Continue an inquiry-based research process by applying critical thinking skills to information and knowledge in order to construct new understandings, draw conclusions, and create new knowledge. | AASL 4.1.7 Use social networks and information tools to gather and share information. |
| --- | --- | --- |
| AASL 4.3.1 Participate in the social exchange of ideas, both electronically and in person. | | |
| ISTE 2A Interact, collaborate, and publish with peers, experts, or others employing a variety of digital environments and media. | ISTE 3B Locate, organize, analyze, evaluate, synthesize, and ethically use information from a variety of sources and media. | ISTE 2C Communicate information and ideas effectively to multiple audiences using a variety of media and formats. |
| | ISTE 4A Identify and define authentic problems and significant questions for investigation. | |

INDICATORS

| Observation, self-reporting and pre- and post-surveys | Interviews and pre- and post-surveys | Product evidence |
| --- | --- | --- |

Adults older than the 18–24 year-old range may very well be interested in participating in a club such as this that creates a supported environment of making. If working with younger students, teen or adult mentors may need to be assigned to each group for their independent work.

# Class Size and Teams

The club encourages independent and complex investigation, so team member composition might include researchers, designers, programmers, videographers, and information specialists. Typically up to four participants per robot, or per team, may be kept actively engaged. For the first four level-one challenges, instructors may wish to provide a robot for every two students if possible, so that all can be physically involved.

Team selection may be a delicate subject. In the first challenge, teams are selected at random. This is to give all a chance to get to know each other a bit before settling in. Teams may be realigned in the first four weeks, but permanent teams will need to be established by week 5. Facilitators may assign teams based on strengths each member can bring to the group, or participants may self-select teams. One way to allow some self-selection, but avoid hurt feelings, is to ask participants to complete a draft card after the first or second week. Ask participants to write down one or two participants with whom they would like to team and, if applicable, one or two participants with whom they would not like to team. Coaches may then assign teams, taking preferences into consideration, as well as skill sets and personalities.

## Mentors and Community Involvement

Because the club activities are independently driven and complex, each team may benefit from a mentor. The mentors may be staff members or volunteers. Libraries using external experts as club facilitators might involve library staff as mentors to provide research support, collaboration coaching, equipment and space access. The club as a whole might also have technical mentors such as local engineers, web designers, and computer programmers who may be brought in to assist teams as needed. Additionally, some challenges require involvement from the community, either as clients to inspire custom robot prototypes, or as resources to provide background about community need.

## Robots

The club activities are intended to stretch participants' ability to create and innovate, so for the full experience, robots need to be able to be built and adapted for unique situations. LEGO® MINDSTORMS® with or without TETRIX®, VEX® IQ, and VEX® EDR all work beautifully. While VEX® PRO and high-end metal robots may be overkill, they will certainly work, and competition teams may use the club activities as off-season practice for custom building and programming. Those using less adaptable robots, such as Sphero or Cubelets, may find that a few of the challenges are within reach with some modification.

## Props and Materials

Beyond robots, the items most needed are resources that most libraries already possess such as books, computers, a strong Internet connection, and group meeting space(s). The game board, team markers, and badge icons are used to track each teams' progress. All three items are printable from the collection of online resources linked in the Appendix. Some libraries may also choose to create physical badges or certificates, but it is not essential.

The in-club badge challenges require:

- Large white paper
- Black tape or permanent marker
- Styrofoam cups, Popsicle sticks, and rubber bands
- Small dolls or figurines (representing the lion)
- Sturdy chairs, stools, or benches

Students will also be required to document their experiences, ideally sharing these reflections in an online environment. Libraries may wish to provide digital cameras, video cameras, notebooks, pens, and pencils to assist with this process.

# Guide Components

In this guide, not all badges include the same elements, but all include some traditional literacy components such as a reading selection or research component, a technology literacy component, and opportunities for communication, critical thinking and problem solving, creativity, and collaboration.

## Traditional Literacy

The activities in this club are based on events in L. Frank Baum's *The Wonderful Wizard of Oz*. The rights to this text have passed into the public domain. There are, however, numerous print, film, and audio productions of the story that retain some manner of copyright. Free to use copies of the original text are available to print, read in browser or on a device, from sources such as Project Gutenberg. As in the other guides, a foundational reading from the text will precede each badge brief announcement. It is common for students to want to read the book in its entirety either in class or at home. Instructors are encouraged to provide copies for checkout and may also wish to highlight other offerings from the library's collection such as the rest of the Land of Oz series, related fiction and nonfiction books and movies.

## Badges and Levels

Rather than by *challenges*, this guide is organized by *badges*. Each badge includes one or more components that may include building, programming, research, and production. In the first meetings of the club, the badges are at a lower, introductory skill-building level and require fewer components. Some teams may be able to earn more than one of these level-one badges at a single meeting. As the club continues, the badge challenges become more difficult. Level-two badges may be earnable in a two-hour club session, whereas level-three badges require more extensive work including research in and about the community.

The badge brief will indicate the components that teams need to complete to earn it. To receive a badge for any challenge, a team must demonstrate the desired level of creativity, critical thinking, problem solving, communication, and collaboration. The team's online journal becomes a significant component in more advanced badges. As teams complete badges, they advance on the yellow brick road toward the Emerald City.

# Introduction: Welcome to Oz

At the first session of the club, these activities help orient participants to the structure of the club, robots, and each other. After welcoming participants to the club, explain that they will be working in teams to solve problems based on events in *The Wizard of Oz*. As most participants will probably be aware, at the beginning of the story Dorothy is transported to Oz by a tornado. Students may not be aware, however, that the same conditions that cause tornadoes have also been known to cause golf ball–sized hail! While even small hail can cause major injury and damage, the upcoming activity will not, and it is sure to be fun and help participants break the ice. Even if participants already know each other on some level, such as from school, beginning with an icebreaker can help breakthrough barriers and redefine relationships in the safe space of the club.

## *Hailing All Teammates!*

Prior to the first session, gather enough scrap paper to give each participant a sheet. Mark each paper with a letter. The quantity of letters should align with the number of teams or robots, that is, if there will be four teams of four people each, four sheets will be marked with the letter *A*, four with the letter *B*, and so on.

Give each student a piece of scrap paper. Ask each to write down the season in which they were born (spring, summer, fall, winter). Have all participants crumple their papers into hailstones. Tell them that, on the count of three, they will (gently) toss their paper balls into the air and then each person will grab the hailstone closest to him/her. If a participant finds, upon opening the hailstone, that the season is the same as her own, she holds on to the hailstone. If not, she will crumple it back up and launch again. Continue until everyone has a hailstone.

After exchanging hailstones, have everyone in a season come together. Ask them to come up with one adjective that describes every member of the group. For instance, all members might be *smart*, or *hungry*. Have students add to the hailstones that they received with this team adjective and a personal choice of *lion*, *tiger*, or *bear*. Once again, all will launch their hailstones. They will keep tossing until everyone has received their own animal back.

Have each animal group join together, and, as a group, come up with one noun that represents something that all members have in common such as *music* or *skateboard*. Have participants memorize the letter at the top of their papers. After also adding their names, for the last time, participants will launch their papers and continue until they receive the same letter back.

Have all members of the same letter come together at a station. These will be the teams for the first badge challenge. These teams do not need to be permanent; if you would prefer to assign them later, do have each group create a unique team name. They may use the words on their hailstones as inspiration.

## Getting Started

Next, explain to participants that the first few sessions of the club will be used to learn some basics about how to build and program the robots. Ask those with more experience to serve as mentors to their teammates, but encourage them to coach only with their words, so the newbies learn by doing. If a good number have worked with robots before, gather some information about what they have done, and what they are hoping to learn.

## Badge 1: Build a Bot

✚CCSS.ELA-LITERACY.CCRA.SL.2, R.7 ✪AASL 1.1.6, 1.1.9, 3.1.2, 3.2.2 ❖ISTE 6A, 6C, 6D

Before anything else can happen, the robots need to be created. For those using VEX® IQ, or EDR, the Clawbot is a good place to start. If working with LEGO® MINDSTORMS® the Educator Vehicle will work well. If working with more advanced participants or robot construction methods, an original model may be built, but keep in mind that at this point only a very simple robot is needed. For this badge, the robot simply needs to be able to drive forward and back, turn, and be programmed to run autonomously. This is a level-one badge.

# Badge 2: Cyclone Spin

This badge is intended to provide an opportunity for students to learn the basics of the programming environment in which they are working. Instructors may wish to provide an overview of the software or programming language used.

## *Read Together*

Read chapter 1: The Cyclone

## *Badge Brief*

This is a level-one badge with two components.

## Component 1

✚CCSS.ELA-LITERACY.CCRA.SL.1, R.10, W.7 ✪AASL 1.1.4, 1.1.6, 1.1.9 ❖ISTE 3B

Research the term *cyclone*. Is it really interchangeable with *tornado*? Why or why not?

## Component 2

✚CCSS.ELA-LITERACY.CCRA.SL.2, R.7 ✪AASL 1.1.6, 1.1.9, 3.1.2, 3.2.2 ❖ISTE 6A, 6C, 6D

Program the robot to spin like a tornado funnel.

# Badge 3: Follow the Yellow Brick Road

This badge provides an introduction to sensors and the line-following function common to many robots. Instructors may wish to highlight resources from the library collection about the 1939 movie.

# Read Together

Read chapter 2: The Council with the Munchkins and chapter 3: How Dorothy Saved the Scarecrow up through the end of the paragraph that begins with, "There were several roads nearby, but it did not take her long to find the one paved with yellow bricks."

# Badge Brief

This is a level-one badge with two components.

# Component 1

✚CCSS.ELA-LITERACY.CCRA.SL.1, SL.5, R.10 ✪AASL 3.1.2, 3.2.2, 4.3.1❖ISTE 2C

As a group, compare and contrast the events and details of the readings so far with those of the famous 1939 movie. Research movie details as needed. Using a large piece of white poster board, make a line down the center using the black tape to make two columns. One column represents the book, and one column represents the movie. List items in either column to support observations, but be sure not to write too close to the black line.

# Component 2

✚CCSS.ELA-LITERACY.CCRA.SL.2, R.7 ✪AASL 1.1.9, 3.1.2, 3.2.2 ❖ISTE 6A, 6C, 6D

*Challenge:* Work together to program the robot to follow the black line.

*Instructor Tips:* Getting a robot to follow a predetermined course by following a line is a handy trick, and thus, it is a common desire of many programmers. One way to achieve it is to use a light sensor pointed down. The robot may be programmed with a loop to read and respond to reflected light. If the light reflected falls below a midpoint level, the robot angles to the right, if the reflected light reading is above midpoint, the robot angles to the left. As the robot alternates between turning away from the black and then toward the black, it moves steadily, if a little drunkenly, down the line.

# Badge 4: The Scarecrow

This badge introduces external elements and may require custom building and programming.

# Read Together

Overlap with the previous reading. Read from the paragraph in chapter 3 that begins with, "There were several roads nearby, but it did not take her long to find the one paved with yellow bricks," through to the end of the chapter.

# Badge Brief

This is a level-one badge with two components. The first component requires some props. Place a Styrofoam cup upside down and insert the Popsicle stick through the center. Place a rubber band around the stick. Provide each team with one of these models.

## Component 1

+CCSS.ELA-LITERACY.CCRA.SL.1, R.7 ✪AASL 1.1.9, 3.1.2, 3.2.2 ❖ISTE 6A, 6C, 6D

Lift the scarecrow, represented by the rubber band, off the pole, and lower him gently to the ground. Make sure not to knock over either the pole or the cup in the process.

## Component 2

+CCSS.ELA-LITERACY.CCRA.SL.1, SL.5, R.10 ✪AASL 3.1.2, 3.2.2, 4.3.1❖ISTE 2C

*Challenge:* Document your team's efforts to complete the challenge in images and writing. Explain how each member contributed and the process used to select or reject ideas.

*Instructor Tips:* If teams have been finalized, this is a good badge with which to start their team journals. Teams may use a free blogging tool like Google's Blogger, create a Facebook or Tumblr page, or build a website from scratch. Every institution has different rules about privacy and guidelines about asking students under 18 to post online. Take these points into consideration when guiding students. In some situations, it may be preferable to have students create blog posts that remain published. The facilitator can still view these posts with the username and password of the blog account. If teams have not been finalized, the students might create a paper, slide, or video presentation

# Badge 5: The Tin Woodman

This badge requires custom building and programming and encourages students to be as creative as possible.

## Read Together

Read chapter 4: The Road through the Forest and chapter 5: The Rescue of the Tin Woodman.

## Badge Brief

This is first level-two badge. The three components complement each other and should be addressed concurrently. If possible, facilitators should provide each team with access to at least two computers, one computer for programming and another one for research. If teams have not already been finalized, this is the time to do so.

## Component 1

✚CCSS.ELA-LITERACY.CCRA.SL.1, W.8 ✪AASL 1.1.4, 1.1.6, 1.1.9, 2.1.1, 3.1.2, 3.2.2, 3.3.4, 4.1.7, 4.3.1 ❖ISTE 3B, 4A, 6A, 6C, 6D

*Challenge:* Create an original anthropomorphic robot that can make a chopping motion.

*Instructor Tips:* The key phrase in this challenge brief is *original.* There are official manufacturer building guides for humanoid robots built from VEX® IQ and LEGO® MINDSTORMS®. Students may certainly use these and examples from the online community as inspiration, but they must avoid replication of any published robot or significant robot component.

## Component 2

✚CCSS.ELA-LITERACY.CCRA.R.7, R.10, SL.2, W.7, W.8 ✪AASL 1.1.1, 1.1.4, 1.1.6, 2.1.1, 3.1.4, 4.1.7❖ISTE 3B, 4A, 2C

*Challenge:* Research and create an annotated reference list of sources that inspire or inform the anthropomorphic robot. A reader should be able locate each of the sources mentioned and understand why it was selected.

*Instructor Tips:* Instructors may require the list to be formatted according to APA, Chicago, or MLA guidelines and to include a certain number of entries. Doing so encourages students to identify the sources of online information. Though not often required by style manuals, consider asking students to include the direct link to online sources. This may be helpful for them in Component 3.

## Component 3

✚CCSS.ELA-LITERACY.CCRA.W.2, W.6, SL.5 ✪AASL 2.1.6, 3.1.4, 3.3.4, 4.1.7, 4.3.1 ✤ISTE 2A, 3B, 2C

*Challenge:* Through your team's journal, tell the story of your robot's inspiration and creation using images, video, and words. Provide clear building and programming instructions that could be used to replicate your design.

*Instructor Tips:* As the online journals begin and expand, instructors may want to engage colleagues and community members with expertise in writing, web design, photography, and videography.

# Badge 6: Brains, Heart, or Courage

This badge prepares students to consider the specific needs of a client. It requires custom building and programming and extensive creativity and problem solving.

## *Read Together*

Revisit the last five paragraphs of chapter 5: The Rescue of the Tin Woodman, and then continue through to the end of chapter 6: The Cowardly Lion.

## *Badge Brief*

This is a level-two badge. The three components should probably be addressed in a linear fashion, although the team should gather information and prepare for Component 3 throughout the process.

## Component 1

✚CCSS.ELA-LITERACY.CCRA.SL.1, SL.5, R.10, W.2 ✪AASL 1.1.6, 1.1.9, 2.1.1, 3.1.2, 3.2.2, 4.3.1 ✤ISTE 4A, 2C

*Challenge:* As a team, select the Lion, the Tin Woodman, or the Scarecrow as a client. Identity the client's need(s) and strategize a robotic solution to the problem. Create a visual representation of the team's thought process and initial strategy.

*Instructor Tips:* The visual representation may take any form that will help the team stay focused on the question at hand.

## Component 2

✦CCSS.ELA-LITERACY.CCRA.SL.1, W.7, W.8 ✪AASL 1.1.4, 1.1.9, 2.1.1, 3.1.2, 3.2.2, 4.3.1 ❖ISTE 3B, 4A, 6A, 6C, 6D

*Challenge:* Create a robotic solution to address your client's problem, researching elements as needed without plagiarizing others' work.

*Instructor Tips:* As those familiar with the tale will recall, Dorothy's companions do not truly lack the elements that they crave, and the desired traits are all somewhat ethereal in nature. This gives teams a lot of leeway to interpret the challenge and the client need. They may choose a literal solution, for instance, creating a robot that can insert a heart into a cavity, or a more imaginative solution. A cowardly robot might shudder to enter a dark room, but turn on a flashlight and do it anyway, demonstrating its newfound courage.

## Component 3

✦CCSS.ELA-LITERACY.CCRA.W.2, W.6, SL.5 ✪AASL 2.1.6, 3.1.4, 3.3.4, 4.1.7, 4.3.1❖ISTE 2A, 3B, 2C

*Challenge:* Through your team's journal, describe the client's need and the team's process in identifying and solving the problem. Site any sources that helped inspire the final solution. Evaluate how well the final product addresses the client's need. How did the team adjust the process along the way? Include the visual representation from Component 1 and a video of at least one team member explaining how the final solution works.

# Badge 7: Real-World Client

The activities for this level-three badge encourage students to start thinking about how their skills and interests might have real-world applications.

# Client Selection

Prior to announcing this challenge, the facilitator should line up one client per team. This client may be a library staff member looking for a solution to a repetitive task, such as shelving books or refilling toilet paper rolls. A client might be a senior citizen that could use a robot to bring him the appropriate pill at the appropriate time, or a client might be an organization. A local pet shelter might like a robotic solution to feed animals or scoop litter boxes. When considering clients, keep in mind that this is a way for the community to become invested in the club. Including a representative from a local business or a colleague from the school may lead to future financial or intellectual support.

It is important for facilitators to help the clients understand the framework of the club and the scope of the challenge. Teams will be creating prototypes to address the need described by their clients rather than permanent solutions that the client will keep.

# Badge Brief

This is the first level-three badge, and it is rated that highly because of the significant levels of communication, collaboration, critical thinking, and creative problem solving required. It will be important to explain this challenge to the teams prior to their first meeting with the client in order to give the team members time to work on Component 1.

# Component 1

✚CCSS.ELA-LITERACY.CCRA.SL.1, SL.2, W.2, W.7 ✪AASL 1.1.6, 1.1.9, 3.1.2, 3.2.2, 4.3.1 ❖ISTE 4A, 2C

*Challenge:* As a team, strategize for the upcoming client meeting. What questions will you ask to accurately assess the client's need? Will one person lead the interview, or will each member of the team speak? How will you make the client feel welcome and fully heard? How will you capture all that the client is telling you? How will you communicate with the client after the meeting?

# Component 2

✚CCSS.ELA-LITERACY.CCRA.SL.1, R.10, W.2 ✪AASL 1.1.9, 2.1.1, 2.1.6, 3.1.2, 3.1.4, 3.2.2, 3.3.4, 4.3.1 ❖ISTE 2A, 4A, 2C

*Challenge:* As a team, review the information that you've gathered from your client. Prioritize all identified problems and select at least one on which to focus. Develop a preliminary plan and communicate it to your client explaining your rationale. Take any additional client feedback into consideration.

*Instructor Tips:* The client communications may need to run through the club coach depending on the library's policies and the clients selected.

## Component 3

✚CCSS.ELA-LITERACY.CCRA.SL.1, W.7, W.8 ✪AASL 1.1.4, 1.1.9, 2.1.1, 3.1.2, 3.2.2, 4.3.1 ❖ISTE 3B, 4A, 6A, 6C, 6D

*Challenge:* Create a robotic solution to address your client's problem, researching elements as needed without plagiarizing others' work.

*Instructor Tips:* Consider having a reveal day in which clients come back into the club and see the solutions created. This might also be more of a science fair type atmosphere that is open to the public.

## Component 4

✚CCSS.ELA-LITERACY.CCRA.W.2, W.6, SL.5 ✪AASL 2.1.6, 3.1.4, 3.3.4, 4.1.7, 4.3.1 ❖ISTE 2A, 3B, 2C

*Challenge:* Through your team's journal, and/or in a local publication, describe the client's need and the team's process in identifying and solving the problem. Site any sources that helped inspire the final solution. Evaluate how well the final product addresses the client's need. How did the team adjust the process along the way? Include the visual representation from Component 1 and a video of at least one team member explaining how the final solution works.

*Instructor Tips:* Clients may need to be kept anonymous. Consult with both the client and library policymakers about any privacy concerns before beginning the process. Consider encouraging teams to write an article for a local newspaper, or a professional journal.

# Badge 8: Hurdle Hopper

The activities in this badge prepare students to take on larger scale challenges within the community.

# Read Together

Read chapter 7: The Journey to the Great Oz

# Badge Brief

This level-two badge requires simple props to create a deep valley over which the robots must cross. This can easily be done with two chairs, benches, or stools placed at a distance from one another, but take care that the furniture pieces used are sturdy enough to withstand the weight of the robots and are heavy enough to hold their positions fairly well against the jostling of the machinery. It may be wise to mark the position of the furniture on the floor with tape, so that, as programs are tested, the field may be reset accurately each time.

# Component 1

✚CCSS.ELA-LITERACY.CCRA.SL.1 ✪AASL 1.1.4, 1.1.6, 1.1.9, 2.1.1, 3.1.2, 3.2.2, 4.3.1 ❖ISTE 3B, 4A, 6A, 6C, 6D

*Challenge:* Program the robot to get from the top of one chair to the top of the other chair. The robot must place any item that connects one chair to the other. You may gain inspiration from research, but you must avoid directly replicating a solution.

*Instructor Tips:* Participants will most certainly have numerous clarifying questions. Instructors may choose whether the entire program must be autonomous or whether teams may drive the robot for a certain percentage. Instructors may also choose to rule on whether a robot may climb the chairs. Whatever parameters are set it is important that they are communicated clearly and early in the process.

# Component 2

✚CCSS.ELA-LITERACY.CCRA.W.2, W.6, SL.5 ✪AASL 2.1.6, 3.1.4, 3.3.4, 4.1.7, 4.3.1❖ISTE 2A, 3B, 2C

*Challenge:* Through your team's journal, tell the story of your robot's inspiration and creation using images, video, and words. Provide clear building and programming instructions that could be used to replicate your design.

# Badge 9: Community Solution

Building from the previous experiences, this next level-three badge encourages students to use their creativity and problem-solving skills to find innovative approaches to meaningful issues.

## Badge Brief

In contrast with Badge 7, teams self-select the topic of this investigation. Instructors may wish to provide parameters, some sample ideas from which to choose, or a common point of inspiration. For instance, the problem must have been mentioned in a local paper in the last three months.

## Component 1

✚CCSS.ELA-LITERACY.CCRA.SL.1, SL.5, R.10, W.2 ✪AASL 1.1.6, 1.1.9, 2.1.1, 3.1.2, 3.2.2, 4.3.1 ❖ISTE 4A, 2C

*Challenge:* As a team, research three issues currently affecting the local community, and select one for further investigation. Strategize ways to address the issue through technology and document the initial game plan.

## Component 2

✚CCSS.ELA-LITERACY.CCRA.SL.1, R.10, W.2 ✪AASL 1.1.9, 2.1.1, 2.1.6, 3.1.2, 3.1.4, 3.2.2, 3.3.4, 4.3.1 ❖ISTE 2A, 4A, 2C

*Challenge:* As a team, review the information that you've gathered about the community issue. Prioritize all identified problems involved and select at least one on which to focus. Develop a preliminary plan and present it to members of the community. Collect, analyze, and incorporate the community's feedback.

*Instructor Tips:* Depending on the topic chosen, students may present their ideas to a focus group, city council, the school board, or others. Teams may also gather feedback online through community forums and social media. Be sure to consult administrators about any policies that may come into play.

## Component 3

✚CCSS.ELA-LITERACY.CCRA.SL.1, W.7, W.8 ✪AASL 1.1.4, 1.1.9, 2.1.1, 3.1.2, 3.2.2, 4.3.1 ❖ISTE 3B, 4A, 6A, 6C, 6D

*Challenge:* Create a prototype to address the community problem, researching elements as needed without plagiarizing others' work.

## Component 4

✚CCSS.ELA-LITERACY.CCRA.W.2, W.6, SL.5 ✪AASL 2.1.6, 3.1.4, 3.3.4, 4.1.7, 4.3.1 ❖ISTE 2A, 3B, 2C

*Challenge:* Through your team's journal, and/or in a local publication, describe the project experience, and the team's process in identifying the problem and creating a solution. Site any sources that helped inspire the final solution. Evaluate how well the final product addresses the problem. How did the team adjust the process along the way? Include the visual representation from Component 1 and a video of at least one team member explaining how the final solution works.

*Instructor Tips:* Consult with library policymakers before beginning the process about any privacy concerns. If possible, consider encouraging teams to write an article for a local newspaper, or a professional journal.

# Badge 10: Kind Critters

This badge introduces the concept of paying kindness forward and altruism.

## *Read Together*

Read chapter 8: The Deadly Poppy Field and chapter 9: The Queen of the Field Mice.

## *Badge Brief*

This level-two badge requires a prop representing the lion. A small stuffed animal, figurine, or doll will work. Tape out an area on the floor to represent the poppy field.

## Component 1

✚CCSS.ELA-LITERACY.CCRA.SL.1 ✪AASL 1.1.4, 1.1.6, 1.1.9, 2.1.1, 3.1.2, 3.2.2, 4.3.1 ❖ISTE 3B, 4A, 6A, 6C, 6D

*Challenge:* Save the lion! Using the field mice as inspiration, move the lion onto a cart and roll him out of harm's way.

## Component 2

✚CCSS.ELA-LITERACY.CCRA.W.2, W.6, SL.5 ✪AASL 2.1.6, 3.1.4, 3.3.4, 4.1.7, 4.3.1❖ISTE 2A, 3B, 2C

*Challenge:* Through your team's journal, tell the story of your robot's inspiration and creation using images, video, and words. Provide clear building and programming instructions that could be used to replicate your design.

# Badge 11: Helping Hand

This badge extends the idea of helping others in the community. Instructors may wish to consider ways in which the club members might contribute to library initiatives in meaningful ways. Are their robotics camps or classes coming up for younger students? Could students use their developing storytelling abilities to document an upcoming library event? Ideally, teams will identify and self-select an opportunity that feels personally relevant, but they may also welcome suggestions.

## *Badge Brief*

This level-three badge does not necessarily require any building or programming, although those elements may be involved. Participants will find or create an outreach opportunity such as leading a basic robotics class for younger students or helping library customers with downloadable collections and tablets. This event should be live, preferably in person, but a webinar with registered attendees may also be an option.

## Component 1

✚CCSS.ELA-LITERACY.CCRA.SL.1, SL.5, W.2, W.7 ✪AASL 1.1.4, 1.1.6, 1.1.9, 1.4.2, 2.1.1, 3.1.2, 3.2.2, 4.3.1 ❖ISTE 4A, 3B, 2C

*Challenge:* As a team, create a list of some of the skills, talents, and abilities you've used in the club. Research some upcoming community events and discuss how your team might be able to support them, or what event is missing from the community calendar that your group might be able to offer. Create a document prioritizing and summarizing your ideas, and consult with the club coach and/or the team's mentor.

## Component 2

+CCSS.ELA-LITERACY.CCRA.SL.1, R.10, W.2 ✪AASL 1.1.9, 2.1.1, 2.1.6, 3.1.2, 3.1.4, 3.2.2, 3.3.4, 4.3.1 ❖ISTE 2A, 4A, 2C

*Challenge:* As a team, review your ideas and integrate your coach's feedback. Select one idea and develop a preliminary plan to develop and present it to the members of the club. Collect, analyze, and incorporate the club's feedback and evaluate opportunities for partnership with other teams.

*Instructor Tips:* This is a great opportunity for two or more teams to work together. By this point, the club should be developing a sense of pride, and teams will be representing the whole club in the community at these events, so it is important that teams feel comfortable with each other's ideas.

## Component 3

+CCSS.ELA-LITERACY.CCRA.SL.1, W.2, SL.5 ✪AASL 1.1.9, 2.1.6, 3.1.2, 3.1.4, 3.2.2, 3.3.4, 4.3.1 ❖ISTE 2A, 2C, 4A, 5D, 6A, 6C, 6D

*Challenge:* Create an action plan that includes a way to assess how well the event addressed your goals. Schedule and lead the event.

## Component 4

+CCSS.ELA-LITERACY.CCRA.W.2, W.6, SL.5 ✪AASL 2.1.6, 3.1.4, 3.3.4, 4.1.7, 4.3.1 ❖ISTE 2A, 3B, 2C

*Challenge:* Through your team's journal, and/or in a local publication, describe the project experience, and the team's process in creating and leading it. Site any sources that helped inspire the event. Evaluate how well you felt the event addressed your goals. Include photos and videos from the event.

*Instructor Tips:* Consult with library policymakers before beginning the process about any privacy concerns. If possible, consider encouraging teams to write an article for a local newspaper, or a professional journal.

# Badge 12: Perspective

This is the culminating badge, and may coincide with the last meeting, but consider concluding the club with a social event, such as hosting a pizza party and screening a *Wizard of Oz* movie (after gaining proper permissions of course). Facilitators may also wish to host some type of award ceremony that recognizes both badges achieved and personal accomplishments in collaboration and creativity.

## *Read Together*

Read chapter 10: The Guardian of the Gates.

## *Badge Brief*

The green spectacles change the perspective of all entering the Emerald City. This level-three badge invites each participant to consider how participating in this club has changed his or her outlook.

## Component 1

✚CCSS.ELA-LITERACY.CCRA.SL.1 ✪AASL 1.1.6, 1.1.9, 3.1.2, 3.2.2, 4.3.1

*Challenge:* Individually take some time to reflect on your experiences in the club. What have you learned about robotics, yourself, your teammates, your fellow club members, and your community? As a group, discuss these reflections.

## Component 2

✚CCSS.ELA-LITERACY.CCRA.W.2, W.6, SL.5 ✪AASL 2.1.6, 3.1.4, 3.3.4, 4.1.7, 4.3.1 ❖ISTE 2A, 3B, 2C

*Challenge:* As a team, select some reflections that members are comfortable sharing with the public, and tell the story on the team's online journal in words, pictures, and video. Include any relevant plans and suggestions for future clubs.

## Conclusion

The club model may be one of the most ambitious ways to integrate robotics learning into libraries and an effective way to build communication and collaboration skills, but we have also seen that one-time events and week-long camps can result in significant gains in traditional and technology literacy, and give students opportunities to creatively explore new interests. Libraries have always been a place to imagine and discover, but now as the role of libraries shifts from warehouses of books to community learning centers, we are presented with the unprecedented opportunity to become tour guides in a vibrant technology-powered landscape. Using robots as traditional literacy tools creates a bridge between worlds and helps students gain the reading, writing, speaking, listening, and information literacy skills that they will need to thrive as digital citizens.

Libraries strive to invest in the right tools at the right time for the right purpose. We buy egg shakers for storytime to help young children physically engage with the phonological rhythms of language. We lease professional development databases to help adults build career skills, and we provide computers, printers, and fax machines for seniors to complete their taxes. What should we select next? Well, years ago, we only needed to help customers use computers because we'd replaced our card catalogs with them. Now, we offer our customers banks of public computers and everything from computer basics to Microsoft® Office classes to digital media creation, and the importance of technology in personal and professional life is not slowing down anytime soon. Code.org predicts that there will be about 1 million more computer science jobs than prepared students to fill them by 2020, representing about $500 billion in opportunity (Code.org, 2015), but this does not even take into account how many of us will use coding in everyday life as we now use technology in ways we would have never predicted even 10 years ago. The right tool right now is one that can prepare customers for a future in which they'll need to understand programming and deeper technology concepts, communicate effectively through written and spoken language skills, participate fully in collaborations of diverse people, navigate an ever-evolving world of digital content and create new knowledge. It is the right time for robots.

Throughout this book, we have explored how we can design classes that help students build the skills found in the Common Core State Standards for English Language Arts and Literacy, the American Association for School Librarians' Standards for the 21st Century Learner, and the International Society for Technology in Education's Standards for Students. The activity guides provided herein offer replicable examples, but the opportunities to use robotics to create multiliteracy learning environments extend far beyond these pages. As we encourage our students to think creatively, problem solve challenges and think critically through obstacles, let us do the same to bring them the tools and skills of the future. Let's bring them robots.

# Appendix

**Robot Jungle Resources**
www.gigalearnit.com/LibraryRobotics/RobotJungle

**Follow the White Rabbit Resources**
www.gigalearnit.com/LibraryRobotics/WhiteRabbit

**Yellow Brick Quest Resources**
www.gigalearnit.com/LibraryRobotics/YellowBrick

# Notes

## Chapter One

1. *Merriam Webster's Collegiate Dictionary*, 11th Ed. s.v.v "literacy," "literate."
2. ISTE Standards for Students, Second Edition, ©2007, ISTE ® (International Society for Technology in Education), iste.org. All rights reserved. Reprinted with permission.
3. Excerpted from *Standards for the 21st-Century Learner* by the American Association of School Librarians, a division of the American Library Association, copyright ©2007 American Library Association. Available for download at www.ala.org/aasl/standards. Reprinted with permission.
4. Excerpted from *Standards for the 21st-Century Learner* by the American Association of School Librarians, a division of the American Library Association, copyright ©2007 American Library Association. Available for download at www.ala.org/aasl/standards. Reprinted with permission.
5. ISTE Standards for Students, Second Edition, ©2007, ISTE ® (International Society for Technology in Education), iste.org. All rights reserved. Reprinted with permission.
6. ISTE Standards for Students, Second Edition, ©2007, ISTE ® (International Society for Technology in Education), iste.org. All rights reserved. Reprinted with permission.
7. ISTE Standards for Students, Second Edition, ©2007, ISTE ® (International Society for Technology in Education), iste.org. All rights reserved. Reprinted with permission.
8. Excerpted from *Standards for the 21st-Century Learner* by the American Association of School Librarians, a division of the American Library Association, copyright ©2007 American Library Association. Available for download at www.ala.org/aasl/standards. Reprinted with permission.
9. ISTE Standards for Students, Second Edition, ©2007, ISTE ® (International Society for Technology in Education), iste.org. All rights reserved. Reprinted with permission.

10. Excerpted from *Standards for the 21st-Century Learner* by the American Association of School Librarians, a division of the American Library Association, copyright ©2007 American Library Association. Available for download at www.ala.org/aasl/standards. Reprinted with permission.

# Chapter Two

1. Christy Cochran (Murchison Middle School Library and Information Specialist), in discussion with the author, December 5, 2014.
2. Ryan Paulsen (New Rochelle High School Library Media Specialist), in discussion with the author, December 5, 2014.
3. Beth Barrett (Director of Library and Museum Services for Louisville, Colorado) in discussion with the author, December 9, 2014.
4. Tod Colegrove (Head of DeLaMare Science and Engineering Library at the University of Nevada, Reno) in discussion with the author, December 11, 2014.
5. Tara Radniecki (Engineering Library, DeLaMare Science and Engineering Library at the University of Nevada, Reno) in discussion with the author, December 11, 2014.
6. Michael Cherry (Teen and Youth Services Librarian, Evansville Vanderburgh Public Library) in discussion with the author, December 5, 2014.
7. Kelly Czarnecki (Teen Services Librarian, ImaginOn, Charlotte Mecklenberg Library) in discussion with the author, December 10, 2014.
8 Christy Cochran (Murchison Middle School Library and Information Specialist), in discussion with the author, December 5, 2014.
9. Beth Barrett (Director of Library and Museum Services for Louisville, Colorado) in discussion with the author, December 9, 2014.
10. Bob Loftin (Municipal Reference Librarian, Plano Public Library) in discussion with the author, December 19, 2014.
11. Michael Cherry (Teen and Youth Services Librarian, Evansville Vanderburgh Public Library) in discussion with the author, December 5, 2014.
12 Tara Radniecki (Engineering Library, DeLaMare Science and Engineering Library at the University of Nevada, Reno) in discussion with the author, December 11, 2014.
13. Megan Alabaugh (Teen Librarian, Rocky River Public Library) in discussion with the author, November 6, 2014.
14. Michael Cherry (Teen and Youth Services Librarian, Evansville Vanderburgh Public Library) in discussion with the author, December 5, 2014.
15. See note 3 above.
16. Ryan Paulsen (New Rochelle High School Library Media Specialist), in discussion with the author, December 5, 2014.
17. Ryan Paulsen (New Rochelle High School Library Media Specialist), in discussion with the author, December 5, 2014.
18. Michael Cherry (Teen and Youth Services Librarian, Evansville Vanderburgh Public Library) in discussion with the author, December 5, 2014.
19. Tad Douce (National Robotics Challenge Director of Events and Tri-Rivers Educational Computer Association Director of Innovation and Development) in conversation with the author, December 17, 2014.
20. Ryan Paulsen (New Rochelle High School Library Media Specialist), in discussion with the author, December 5, 2014.

21. Christy Cochran (Murchison Middle School Library and Information Specialist), in discussion with the author, December 5, 2014.
22. Bob Loftin (Municipal Reference Librarian, Plano Public Library) in discussion with the author, December 19, 2014.
23. Amy (Stafford) Georgopoulous (Youth Services Librarian, Haslet Public Library) in conversation with the author, December 15, 2014
24. Michael Cherry (Teen and Youth Services Librarian, Evansville Vanderburgh Public Library) in discussion with the author, December 5, 2014.

## Chapter Three

1. Heather Booth (Teen Services Librarian, Thomas Ward Memorial Library and member of The Robot Test Kitchen) in conversation with the author, December 18, 2014.
2. Douglas Adams, *The Salmon of Doubt: Hitchhiking the Galaxy One Last Time* (digital edition, Random House Publishing Group, 2005), "The Universe: Build It and We Will Come."
3. Sharon Hrycewicz (Children's Reference and Technology Coordinator, Downer's Grove Public Library, and member of the Robot Test Kitchen) in conversation with the author, December 18, 2014.
4. Jacquie Christen (Grade School Program Coordinator, Glenside Public Library and member of The Robot Test Kitchen) in conversation with the author, December 18, 2014.
5. Bob Loftin (Municipal Reference Librarian, Plano Public Library) in discussion with the author, December 19, 2014.
6. See note 3 above.
7. See note 1 above.
8. Kimberly Calkins (Middle School Services Librarian, Elmhurst Public Library and member of the Robot Test Kitchen) in discussion with the author, December 18, 2014.
9. Stephan Turnipseed (LEGO® Education President Emeritus and Executive Director of Strategic Partnerships) in discussion with the author, January 16, 2015.
10. Ryan Paulsen (New Rochelle High School Library Media Specialist) in discussion with the author, December 5, 2014.

# Glossary

**activities.**   What participants in an initiative will do to progress toward outcomes.

**anchor standards.**   Central concepts of a standards system (such as the Common Core State Standards) that may be developed more specifically for each grade level.

**Bee-Bot™.**   A plastic shelled robot product that resembles a bumblebee.

**Connected Learning.**   The educational philosophy and practice of intertwining social experience, academic content, and individual interests into a personal learning network.

**Cubelets.**   Magnetic blocks, each containing mechanical parts and programming that when used together can form a robot.

**Flipped Learning.**   The educational philosophy and practice of assigning students the homework of watching video-recorded lessons, and then using classroom time for projects, collaboration, coaching, and interactivity.

**gamification.**   The utilization of game elements (such as levels, points, and rewards) to increase engagement.

**impact.**   What an initiative will accomplish overall.

**indicator.**   Tools to provide evidence to the extent to which a certain outcome has or has not been achieved.

**input.**   Resources delivered to or consumed by the initiative.

**outcome.**   The measureable goals of an initiative.

**output.**   A direct product of an initiative's activities.

**LEGO® MINDSTORMS®.**   A robotics system from LEGO® company consisting of kits with LEGO® pieces, sensors, curriculum, and software. It has included three iterations, the RCX, NXT, and EV3.

**LEGO® WeDo®.**   A robotics system from LEGO® company consisting of kits with LEGO® bricks, sensors, curriculum, and software.

**logic model.**   A graphical tool used to organize an initiative's outcomes, inputs, activities, and outputs.

**machine.**   A device that performs a task when given power.

**robot.**   A machine that is programmable and autonomous or semi-autonomous.

**sensor**.   A device that detects and reports a change in a physical stimulus (such as light, heat, sound).

**STEAM.**   Science, Technology, Engineering, Art, and Math.

**summer slide**.   A term for the loss of knowledge and skills that is believed to happen to students who are not cognitively engaged over the summer.

**technology literacy**.   Relating to technology fluency.

**traditional literacy**.   Relating to language communication dexterity (involving activities such as reading, writing, speaking, and listening)

**21st Century Skills.**   The attributes (such as creativity, communication, collaboration, critical thinking, and problem solving) beyond academic knowledge that students will need to be successful in the 21st century.

**VEX®**.   A fleet of robotics products offered by Innovation First International, INC. that includes VEX® IQ, VEX® EDR, and VEX® PRO.

# References

American Association of School Librarians. 2007. "Standards for the 21st Century Learner." http://www.ala.org/aasl/standards-guidelines/learning-standards.

Bureau of Labor Statistics, U.S. Department of Labor. May 21, 2014. *The Economics Daily*, "Indiana Has Highest Share of Total Employment in Manufacturing." http://www.bls.gov/opub/ted/2014/ted_20140521.htm.

California Library Association. 2014. "California Summer Reading Program: Value of Summer Reading." http://www.cla-net.org/?78.

Code.org. 2015 "Stats" http://code.org/stats.

Common Core State Standards Initiative. 2014a. *College and Career Readiness Anchor Standards for Speaking and Listening*, "Note on Range and Content of Student Speaking and Listening." http://www.corestandards.org/ELA-Literacy/CCRA/ SL/Cullinan, Bernice. 2000. *School Library Media Research* 3, "Independent Reading and School Achievement." http://www.ala.org/aasl/sites/ala.org.aasl/ files/content/aaslpubsandjournals/slr/vol3/SLMR_IndependentReading_V3.pdf.

FIRST: About Us. 2014. "Gracious Professionalism." http://www.usfirst.org/aboutus/ gracious-professionalism.

FIRST LEGO® League. 2014. *Challenges & Resources*. "Participation Rules." http:// www.firstlegoleague.org/challenge/participationrules.

Graham, Steve and Michael Hebert. 2010. *Writing to Read: Evidence for How Writing Can Improve. Carnegie Corporation Time to Act Report*. Washington, DC: Alliance for Excellent Education. Accessed August 8, 2015 https://www .carnegie.org/publications/writing-to-read-evidence-for-how-writing- can-improve-reading/.

Howard, Christina and Alex Holcomb. 2010. "Unexpected Changes in Direction of Motion Attract Attention." *Attention, Perception, & Psychophysics* 72, no. 8: 2087–95. Accessed October 20, 2014. http://www.psych.usyd.edu.au/staff/alexh/ research/papers/HowardHolcombe_APP_2010.pdf.

International Society of Technology in Education. 2007. "ISTE Standards for Students, Second Edition." http://www.iste.org/standards.

LEGO®. "History of LEGO Robotics." http://www.lego.com/en-us/mindstorms/history.

Lexile® Framework for Reading. 2015. "Find a Book."

Kurzweil, Ray. 2001. "The Law of Accelerating Returns." http://www.kurzweilai.net/the-law-of-accelerating-returns.

Markel, Howard. April 22, 2011. "The Origin of the Word Robot." *Science Diction*. National Public Radio. http://www.npr.org/2011/04/22/135634400/science-diction-the-origin-of-the-word-robot.

New York State Library. August 14, 2014. "The Importance of Summer Reading: Public Library Summer Reading Programs and Learning." http://www.nysl.nysed.gov/libdev/summer/research.htm#bibliography.

Robinson, Ken. 2006. February. "Ken Robinson Says Schools Kill Creativity." TED. http://www.ted.com/talks/ken_robinson_says_schools_kill_creativity.html.

Robotics Education & Competition Foundation. 2014. "VRC Teams" http://www.roboticseducation.org/vex-robotics-competitionvrc/vrc-team-leadercoach/

Scholastic Teachers. 2015. "*Alice in Wonderland* by Lewis Carroll | Scholastic.com." http://www.scholastic.com/teachers/book/alice-wonderland#cart/cleanup.

Search Institute. 2015. "40 Developmental Assets for Adolescents." Accessed August 8, 2015. http://www.search-institute.org/research/developmental-assets

Tanglao, Leezel. April 8, 2014. "New York School Librarian Leads Robotics Club to Compete in Robots Competition." *School Library Journal*.

United States Department of Education. 2010. "National Education Technology Plan Executive Summary- Transforming American Education: Learning Powered by Technology 2010." http://www.ed.gov/sites/default/files/netp2010-execsumm.pdf.

University of Texas at Austin: Mechanical Engineering. March 8, 2011. "DTEACh Overview." http://www.me.utexas.edu/news/2011/0311_dteach.php.

# Bibliography

American Association of School Librarians. "Learning Standards & Common Core State Standards Crosswalk." http://www.ala.org/aasl/standards-guidelines/crosswalk.

Connected Learning. "Connected Learning Infographic." http://connectedlearning.tv/infographic.

Connected Learning Alliance. http://clalliance.org/.

Flipped Learning Network. http://flippedlearning.org.

Kipling, Rudyard. *The Jungle Book*. New York: Random House, 2012.

Kipling, Rudyard, Don Daily, and Elizabeth Encarnacion. *The Jungle Book*. The Classic Edition, first ed. Kennebunkport: Cider Mill Press, 2014.

McGonigal, Jane. *Reality Is Broken: Why Games Make Us Better and How They Can Change the World*. New York: Penguin Press, 2011.

Partnership for 21st Century Skills. "Framework for 21st Century Learning." http://www.p21.org/our-work/p21-framework.

Teaching the Core: A Non-Freaked Out Approach to Literacy, Common Core or Otherwise. "The Best of Teaching the Core." http://www.teachingthecore.com/best-of-teaching-the-core/.

# Index

Note: Page numbers in *italics* followed by *f* indicate figures and by *t* indicate tables